Winning Grants
Step by Step

Winning Grants Step by Step

The **Complete Workbook** for **Planning, Developing,** and **Writing Successful Proposals** | FIFTH EDITION

Tori O'Neal-McElrath | Lynn Kanter | Lynn English

WILEY

Library of Congress Cataloging-in-Publication Data is Available:
ISBN 9781119547341 (Paperback)
ISBN 9781119547372 (ePDF)
ISBN 9781119547365 (ePub)

Cover Design: Wiley
Cover Image: © Theerapan Bhumirat/Getty Images

Printed in the United States of America

SKY10024535_012821

Contents

List of Figures, Samples, and Worksheets

Acknowledgments

THE FIRST EDITION of this workbook was created and written in 1995 by Mim Carlson, leadership transition coach and former executive director of several nonprofits in northern California. Her strategic, tried-and-true approach to the first *Winning Grants* workbook created the template upon which each of the following editions has been built.

The approach taken for this edition was that "three veteran fundraising practitioners are better than one." Accordingly, two creative and highly successful fundraising consultants (Lynn English and Lynn Kanter) joined forces with Tori O'Neal-McElrath as co-authors.

This workbook is a coming together of all aspects of the winning grants process: prospect research, program planning, grantwriting, proposal submission and follow up, as well as relationship building and stewardship. In this fifth edition, *Winning Grants Step by Step* will continue to augment the many workshops and clinics, as well as the various other forms of consultation available on grantseeking and grantwriting.

Readers will also find new information not available in any of the previous *Winning Grants* editions relative to public funding and navigating the online proposal submission process.

Special thank yous to our families, friends, and colleagues who supported us along our journey of creating *Winning Grants, Step by Step, Fifth Edition*.

About the Authors

TORI O'NEAL-MCELRATH has nearly three decades of executive-level experience in external affairs and organizational development with a broad range of nonprofit organizations and foundations. Since 2015, Tori has served as the vice president of external affairs at Demos, a national think-and-do tank that produces cutting-edge policy research, inspiring litigation and deep relationships with grassroots organizations, for the purpose of championing solutions that will create a democracy and economy rooted in racial equity. Prior to Demos, she served for seven years as the director of institutional advancement at Community Change. Tori was also the founding principal of O'Neal Consulting, an organizational development practice that specialized in fundraising, strategic planning, multi-funder collaborations, board development, and interim executive leadership. She was a contributing author to *Nonprofit 101: A Complete and Practical Guide for Leaders and Professionals*, as well as the author of the third and fourth of editions of *Winning Grants, Step by Step*.

Lynn English is a development consultant who has served as a fundraising executive and consultant for dozens of nonprofit organizations across the country and internationally. She has over two decades of experience in proposal writing for foundations, corporations, and local, state and federal agencies – representing everything from small start-up programs to multimillion-dollar national initiatives. She also provides trainings, workshops, and coaching on the proposal writing process. Lynn holds a BA in English from Georgetown University and an MA in English literature from the University of Maryland at College Park.

Lynn Kanter has worked as a writer and fundraiser for nonprofit organizations for more than 25 years. Serving primarily as a grant proposal writer, she has helped raise over $100 million for nonprofits in the social justice field. As the writing director for Community Change, a national nonprofit focused on building power in low-income communities of color, she handled complex, multimillion-dollar proposals, and trained and led a team of proposal writers. Since 2016, she has worked as a consultant, writing for national nonprofit organizations. Lynn is the author of three published novels.

How to Use This Workbook

WINNING GRANTS STEP BY STEP, Fifth Edition, takes the grantseeker on a practical, step-by-step journey through the grantwriting process, illustrating the importance of research on the front end, following the directions provided by each prospective funder, building relationships, and conducting solid program planning as the keys – the steps – to winning grants. Implementing the strategies as outlined, grantseekers will significantly increase their ability to present their organization's programs and general operating needs in compelling proposals worthy of funder consideration. This workbook is the blueprint to creating winning grants.

This is a hands-on, user-friendly guide that helps grantseekers through every important step of proposal development that will enable organizations to take an idea or concept from its inception to a fully fleshed-out proposal:

- Real-life examples, material samples, and worksheets specific to each step will support the grantseeker through every step as they create their proposals.

- Guidelines, suggestions, guiding questions, and exercises specific to each step prepare the grantseeker to tackle proposal development for various organizations in the nonprofit arena.

- Reality Checks and Helpful Hints offer focused guidance.

- Definitions help demystify nonprofit terms that may not be familiar to the grantseeker.

Something brand new in this edition, *Winning Grants Step by Step, Fifth Edition*, incorporates strategies and guidance specific to public funding.

This workbook has a companion website, www.wiley.com/go/winning grants5e, that contains all the worksheets found at the end of chapters, as well as live links to the references provided in Resource C (Resources for Grantseekers). Readers are encouraged to refer to the companion website to use the worksheets in conjunction with developing proposals and letters of inquiry to meet the requirements of funding institutions of various types – community, corporate, family, operating, and private.

Winning Grants Step by Step, Fifth Edition is crafted with four kinds of individuals in mind:

1. Entry-level grantwriters

2. Other organizational staff and volunteers with limited knowledge and/or experience with grantwriting

3. People with some experience who are seeking a refresher in Grantwriting 101

4. People interested in pursuing public-funding grants

Grantwriting basics are applicable to all types of grant processes; however, this workbook's primary focus is on foundation grants, with some limited focus on corporate grants, as well as some new, focused guidance on public funding.

Winning Grants Step by Step, Fifth Edition is direct in its focus: a grant proposal (of any kind) must articulate a well-thought-out, well-crafted program that both inspires confidence in the nonprofit's ability to achieve the stated goals, and fits within the stated interests of the grantmakers who will review it for funding consideration. Funders seek strategic charitable investments with their limited grant resources, and they want to see a direct connection between the organization and its ability to meet community needs. Additionally, they need to understand how organizations plan to track, measure, and report out on their success.

Most organizations addressing community needs have good ideas. The key to winning grants is to match those good ideas, along with a thoughtful programmatic plan complete with goals and objectives, with funders interested in the same ideas, communities, goals, and outcomes.

Step One of this workbook walks grantseekers through developing a proposal idea.

Step Two provides guidance on introducing an organization to possible funders, as well as some helpful ideas on ways to develop relationships with funders, a critical component in winning grants.

Steps Three through Ten focus on the proposal components that will take ideas from concept to winning grant.

Step Eleven walks grantseekers through the final step in the process, which is submitting the proposal.

Step Twelve focuses on how to sustain relationships with funders – whether the proposal was funded or not.

Finally, the Resources section covers prospect research and provides links to directories, guides, tutorials, portals, foundation websites, and other websites that could be helpful to the users of this workbook.

One of the key features of *Winning Grants Step by Step, Fifth Edition* is the sample proposal, with excerpts from the sample incorporated into each chapter to highlight the purpose of each step. The sample proposal focuses on the work of the Alyson Eats organization, whose mission is to reduce hunger in the city of Alyson. The city is fictitious and so is the organization, which is loosely based on a similar program targeting food insecurity.

It is important to emphasize that the most effective way to use *Winning Grants Step by Step, Fifth Edition* is to go through it *step by step*, crafting a grant proposal along the way and using the worksheets as a guide. This workbook is unique in that it is structured to follow a process typically used when preparing a grant proposal.

There is no secret or shortcut to navigating the grantseeking process and winning grants. It is all about implementing a process that has solid planning, clear writing, strong research, and an approach that is tailored to the funder with whom you have developed a good relationship.

Public Funding

In this edition of *Winning Grants*, we have added information about pursuing public funding – grants from federal, state, and local agencies and entities, and other governmental or quasi-governmental organizations. The information provided herein is primarily intended to help new grantseekers understand the differences and similarities between public funding applications and those prepared for foundation and corporate funders, and to provide resources where grantseekers can find more information on this distinct area of grantwriting. We have provided a list of good resources for developing public-funding proposals in the Resource section.

Helpful Hint

HOW TO STAY WITHIN THE LENGTH LIMITS FUNDERS REQUIRE

Many grant proposals are submitted through online portals, and in most cases these portals limit text to a certain length. For instance, the evaluation section could be limited to 3,000 characters, including spaces.

Use the word-count feature that most word processing programs have to find out how long the evaluation section is. If the section has been written as concisely as possible but is still too long, whittle down the words. This is an effective way to shorten text, a few characters at a time. Here are a few tips, most of which are also helpful to strengthen writing in general.

Excise double descriptions. Look for places where two descriptors were used but one will suffice, for example, "The work is both challenging and demanding." Choose one and delete the other. Be ruthless.

Delete flabby words. In good writing, every word must carry its weight; if a word doesn't provide important meaning to the reader, you don't need it. Certain words are generally suspect. For instance, the words *key* and *specific* should be used sparingly. These are good words to delete if they are not absolutely necessary to the reader's understanding. So is *absolutely,* for that matter! Same with *successfully*: If a program successfully increased participation by 50 percent, a grantwriter can communicate that just as well without using *successfully* – and save 12 characters.

Replace words or phrases with shorter ones. Approximately 3,000 can become *about 3,000,* and shave off 8 characters.

Consider cutting words that end in -ly. Many words that end in *-ly* are adverbs: words that further describe other words. Most sentences, although not all, are just as good without them. Strongly, honestly, swiftly – delete them whenever possible. It's also good to cut (or avoid in the first place) words that intensify other words, such as *very* and *extremely.*

Bend some rules. It's fair to take some shortcuts to save space, even if they would not necessarily be appropriate in a full-length text. Use a numeral instead of spelling out a number; replace *percent* with %. Use a well-known acronym instead of writing out a full name.

Introduction
An Overview of the Grantseeking Process

FOUNDATION GRANTS ARE AN ESSENTIAL part of nearly every nonprofit organization's funding mix. Regardless of organizational size, most nonprofits depend on grants as a source of revenue. On its face, it appears that grants take less effort than individual giving and yield larger rewards. In many respects, this is true. However, it is important to note that although grantseeking (prospecting/research, inquiry, proposal writing, submission) is relatively inexpensive in comparison to other revenue-generating strategies from an investment/rewards standpoint, and it does tend to yield larger award amounts, there are expenses associated with it that should not be overlooked.

To be successful in winning grants, an organization must dedicate a significant amount of staff time – and possibly secure the services of an external consultant – for prospect research, program planning, budgeting, collection of required supporting materials, and attention to details and various deadlines. A solid proposal (well-written, well-organized, and concise) can potentially secure solid income for organizational and programs operations.

Who needs to be involved in the grantseeking process? This is an important question, as the more clarity and attention to detail in the grantseeking process, the greater the odds for a stronger, more compelling proposal. Here are some of the key players in the grantseeking process:

1. *Lead program staff*: If the grant proposal is for a specific program (new or expansion of an existing program), the lead staff person of said program is a must. This person is responsible for providing a coherent program plan that articulates the details for Steps 3 (problem statement), 4 (goals and objectives), and 5 (strategies) of the winning grant proposal development. If an organization lacks fundraising staff

and/or the resources to secure an external grantwriting consultant, the program staff person may also serve as the point of contact with prospective funders, as well as the grantwriter for the proposal.

2. *Finance person*: This person might be on staff or an external consultant, and is an essential component for Steps 7 (sustainability) and 8 (program budget) of the winning grant-proposal process. This person is responsible for the budgetary articulation of the written proposal, as well as the approver of all anticipated expenditures necessary to implement the winning grant, should it be awarded to the organization.

3. *Grantwriting consultant*: If an organization does not have fundraising staff, it may need to retain the services of a professional grantwriting consultant, should financial resources be available to do so. This might prove even more necessary when pursuing public funding, which can be quite labor-intensive and exacting in terms of grant guidelines and submission requirements. The grantwriting consultant is responsible for writing the proposal. This means that there will still need to be staff capacity dedicated to managing the submission process (timeline, communication with the funder, gathering needed supporting materials, vetting the proposal with all necessary internal stakeholders, etc.).

4. *Executive director*: For some organizations, the executive director and program staff person are one and the same. For organizations in which this is not the case, the executive director should be brought in to: (1) sign off on the front end of the pursuit of funding specific to the program or project being targeted, including the program plan developed by the lead program staff person, (2) approve retaining a grantwriting consultant, inclusive of the budgetary expense (if applicable), and (3) sign off on the final proposal, including the corresponding budget and the prospective commitments being made by the organization, should the organization achieve a winning grant. If the proposal is for general support of the organization, the executive director will serve as a key member of the proposal development team.

Reality Check

Not every organization is ready to pursue or receive grant funding. Before an organization invests time and resources into winning grants, or attempts to grow its foundation funding from smaller grants to more substantial funding, the staff and board should ask itself this question: *Is the organization ready for grant funding or a significant increase in grant funding?*

To address that issue, organizational leadership should start by answering these five sets of questions:

1. Are the organization's mission, purpose, and goals already well-established and articulated? Does the organization have its strategic plan or annual operating plan completed? And if yes, are you using it to guide the organization?

2. Does the organization have good financial procedures and systems in place? Does it effectively track, monitor, and report on how it expends both restricted and unrestricted grant funds? Are its 990s and audited financial statements in order?

3. Does the organization have the necessary staff in place to ensure that it can deliver on its stated goals and objectives? If not, does the leadership possess the ability to get the right staff in place should the organization be awarded a grant? Can the organization do what it promises?

4. Is organizational leadership prepared to do what it takes to meet the requirements that come with receiving grant funding? These requirements vary depending on the amount and source of funding and might include some (or all) of the following: producing quarterly, semiannual, or annual progress reports (including financial updates relative to the grant); conducting ongoing program evaluation; participating in special trainings; and attending conferences and/or meetings (particularly if the funding relates to a special initiative of a foundation). Meeting grant expectations might also require the organization to expand its services, increase its office space, and/or expand its support staff (with human resources efforts, information technology, and training).

5. Does the organization have access to, and understanding of, technology? Most foundations have moved to online submission processes. Does the organization have an online presence in the form of a website and/or social media (active Facebook or Twitter platform)? Although not mandatory, most foundations anticipate grantseeking organizations having some sort of online presence, so you should conduct an honest assessment of whether you have the basic technology in place to engage in the grantseeking process online.

If an organization can answer yes to these five groups of questions, it achieves the preliminary benchmark to begin the grantseeking process in earnest.

In many instances, a well-prepared and clearly articulated grant proposal can build an organization's credibility with grantmakers, whether the organization is initially successful in securing funding or not. Funders of all types (public, private, and operating foundations, as well as public funding) are engaging in community and/or issue convenings as a routine part of their work. Participation in these types of convenings is another solid way to engage potential funders.

Grantseeking is the most popular way for nonprofits to secure funding for programs and general operating support; however, it is but one of several ways an organization can raise funds. There are many different fundraising strategies that may generate revenue for an organization, including individual major giving/one-on-one solicitation, email fundraising, social media strategies involving Facebook, Twitter, Instagram, SnapChat, and various other platforms, text/mobile strategies, membership drives, workplace giving, special events, donor giving clubs, "thons" (as in walk-a-thons, dance-a-thons, and jump-a-thons), and more. These strategies should all be kept in mind in addition to grantseeking as a part of a well-rounded fundraising plan. Not only is a diversified fundraising plan something funders encourage, but it is vital to a non-profit's ongoing work, as gaining support is important to build shared ownership in the nonprofit by constituents and other supporters, so it remains wellgrounded.

Something else that is important to keep in mind about grantseeking: *the process takes time*. Some grant cycles take six months or longer from the time a grant proposal is submitted to the time you learn whether it has been funded. If an organization is awarded a grant, it might take another few weeks before funding is received, which is more frequently being sent electronically, as opposed to a paper check. This once again highlights the need for organizations to have appropriate finance protocols and technology in place.

Nonprofit organizations have experienced significant shifts in the funding climate over the past several years, but one thing remains the same, particularly for larger organizations: most of the funds raised in the private sector come from individuals, not foundations. The chart in Figure I.1 illustrates this point.

FIGURE I.1
2017 Contributions: $410.02 Billion by Source of Contributions (in billions of dollars – all figures are rounded)

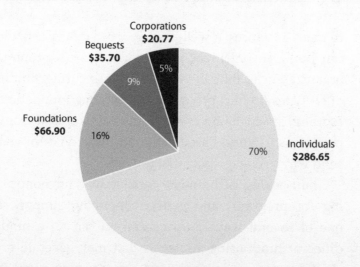

Source: Giving USA Foundation, Giving USA 2017: The Executive Summary of the Annual Report on Philanthropy for the Year 2017.Glenview, IL: Giving USA Foundation, 2018.

Public funding, derived through grants from federal, state, and local agencies, adds billions of public dollars that are not factored into the chart in Figure I.1. That said, public funds are typically aimed at projects with defined target audiences and qualifications, so grantseekers should do their homework to ensure that there is indeed a match worth investing the effort to produce these typically onerous grant proposals – it will most certainly take time and clear intention, not to mention the significant due diligence required to steward this kind of funding once secured.

Reality Check

All foundations are not created equal. Many national foundations direct most of their grants to larger organizations. National nonprofits, including those with chapters or affiliates across the country, major universities, hospitals, and museums are the primary beneficiaries of their support. The good news is that there are literally thousands of local, regional, and statewide foundations that fund various-sized organizations. Smaller and mid-sized foundations are often located in the very communities served by organizations. Therefore, organizations seeking grants should be diligent when conducting prospect research. Do not ignore small and midsized foundations.

Categories of Support

Organizations are dynamic and have varied financial needs, which typically fall into one of the following categories:

- *Operating* (general support, general operating support, or unrestricted income). This funding allows maximum flexibility and can be used wherever the organization deems it most needed. This means it can be used for programmatic purposes, or to pay rent, utilities, and other costs of operating a nonprofit organization. This funding is not restricted to a specific program or service.

- *Program* (temporarily restricted income). Program or special project funding is sometimes of primary interest to grantmakers because some deem it the most quantifiable of grants. It is funding that organizations receive to start a new program, continue operating a program, expand an existing program, or launch a time-limited project.

- *Capacity building*. This funding is used for a targeted effort to increase an organization's capacity to better support its work. Some foundations are willing to invest in building an organization's capacity when said organization demonstrates its value. This time-limited, restricted funding supports things like a website rebuild, fundraising capacity expansion, or strategic planning, as some examples.

- *Capital or equipment.* Funds for capital support are often raised through a targeted fundraising drive known as a capital campaign, or through seeking special equipment grants. These intensive efforts – designed to generate a specified amount of funds within a specified time period for construction, remodeling and renovation, building expansion, or the purchase of land or equipment – typically involve large-scale individual major gift solicitations, followed by substantial support from foundations and corporations.

- *Research.* Funds awarded to institutions to cover costs of investigation and clinical trials. Research grants for individuals are usually referred to as fellowships.

Definitions

Earned income is money received by an organization in return for the sale of a product or rendered service.

Capacity building is the development of an organization's core skills and capabilities, such as leadership, management, finance and fundraising, programs, and evaluation, to build the organization's effectiveness and sustainability.

The Proposal Process

There is no "secret sauce" to writing a winning grant proposal. The keys to success are:

- Documenting an unmet community need, which the grantseeker is positioned to address.

- Developing a clear plan for the program (or operations stability/growth or capital work).

- Researching funders thoroughly.

- Building strong relationships with funders.

- Targeting proposals carefully.

- Writing a concise proposal.

Whether preparing a proposal for a foundation or a corporation, the process of proposal writing will be essentially the same. Organizations will:

- Identify an unmet need that said organization is able to address.

- Determine if other organizations within the community they serve are currently attempting to address this unmet need.

- Develop the plan to meet the need.

- Determine whether there are potential partners or collaborators.
- Identify potential funders and begin to build relationships with them.
- Write the proposals, with each being tailored specifically for one potential funder.
- Engage in strategic follow-up once the proposal has been submitted.

This book covers the proposal process in detail in Steps 1–12. The major components of a proposal are as follows:

- *Cover letter*: a short letter that accompanies the proposal and briefly describes its significance
- *Executive summary* (or proposal summary, summary, abstract): a very brief (usually one page or less) overview of the proposal
- *Problem statement* (or statement of need, need statement): a compelling description of the need to be addressed by the grantseeker
- *Organizational background* (or background statement): a presentation of the nonprofit's qualifications to carry out the proposed project
- *Goals and objectives*: a description of what the organization ultimately hopes to accomplish with a program (goals), and a spelling out of the specific results or outcomes to be achieved during the grant period (objectives)
- *Strategies*: a description of the programs, services, and activities that will achieve the desired results
- *Evaluation*: a plan for assessing program accomplishments
- *Sustainability*: a presentation of the nonprofit's strategies for developing additional funding to continue the program after the initial grant funding is over
- *Budget*: a line-item summary and narrative of program revenues and expenses

A proposal's format and length will vary depending on the grantmaker. In general, proposals contain the same key components to help funders understand that an organization has a sound plan that meets an important need and will make a positive impact on whomever it serves. The format laid out in this book is commonly used among funders but is by no means the only format possible. Highlighted throughout this workbook is the reality that most funders large and small are employing an online portal proposal process. These processes typically limit your ability to go deeper in explanation and details due to space restrictions; however, they still follow to a large degree the step-by-step process outlined in this book.

The step-by-step process is a useful and hands-on way to develop an organization's thoughts and present its program. After you follow these well-defined steps, it will be easier to shift the various components into whatever order individual funders request. The importance of following each grantmaker's guidelines cannot be emphasized enough. These guidelines will walk grantseekers through funders' requirements for proposal development, packaging, and submission.

Types of Proposals

Broadly speaking, there are three types of proposals.

1. A *concept paper* is generally a two-or three-page summary (though some funders may request a specific number of pages) submitted when the funder wishes to see a brief description of the project before deciding whether to ask for a longer, more detailed proposal. This document must focus on how the proposed project fits the priorities of the funder. It should also describe the need and outline the organization's plan to meet it.

2. A *letter proposal* is sometimes requested by corporations. It is typically a three- or four-page description of the project plan, the organization requesting the funds, and the actual request.

3. A *full proposal* is a format that includes a cover letter and a proposal summary, and is the type most often requested by foundations. Corporations should not receive this format unless they specifically request it. Full proposals range in length, as well as in the number of requested attachments. In the longer proposal, you have an opportunity to give substantial details about the project and its importance to the community. This would be a good time to restate that many foundations now employ an online grant submission process, so it is likely that space will be limited.

Tips for Writing Proposals

There are three basic things grantseekers should keep in mind when conceiving their proposals:

1. Picture the readers of your grant as curious, caring, and educated people who may not be knowledgeable of your organization's issue, or don't have a firm grasp on the work of the organization – but they're interested. What are the key things you would share to transfer excitement and a sense of mission?

2. Be sure to use compelling facts. Also, be sure to tell compelling stories that highlight what the organization does, how it does its work, and why it matters. Put a face, place, and situation to the facts to make them real.

3. Always keep in mind that a grant is not just a grant; it is an investment on the part of the funder. Foundations have limited resources and a commitment to advance the foundation's mission. Therefore, it is important to their board and the larger community that they make smart investments.

    Stick to the following principles when preparing the proposal:

-   *Follow the grant guidelines.* You do not want your proposals dismissed on a technicality, which happens more than most grantseekers think. It is common for grantmakers to be explicit about the format they want followed.

-   *Get the facts straight.* Make sure data are relevant and up-to-date to support the need for the program. General data to help set a framework for the statement of need are worthwhile, but the most important data are the facts and figures specific to the geographical area served, target audience, and other key elements.

-   *Do not make your proposal so bleak that the reader sees no point in trying to address the problem.* Use an affirming writing style, and present a well-reasoned, thoughtful presentation. A grant proposal should contain some elements of emotional appeal yet also be realistic and factual.

-   *Be aware that many grantmakers read the proposal summary first, followed closely by the proposal budget.* For this reason, grantseekers should consider developing the proposal summary last.

-   *KISS (Keep It Sweet and Simple).* Make it easy for someone who is not an expert in the field to read, understand, and digest the entire proposal. Jargon (specialized words that only people in the relevant field will understand) is a barrier to understanding, and people cannot be sympathetic to things they cannot comprehend. Be thrifty with words, especially now in the age of online proposals, where word limits are typically in place, but do not sacrifice information that is critical to making the case for the project.

-   *Get some honest feedback on the proposal before submitting it to a funder.* Ask one or two people (maybe a staff or board member or even someone outside your organization) to review the proposal carefully. Does everything make sense? Is the need clear? Do the proposed objectives (Step 4) and strategies (Step 5) seem to be an appropriate response to the identified unmet need? Use the answers to these questions to strengthen the final proposal.

- *Remember that one size does **not** fit all.* After developing a proposal, review the guidelines of each prospective funder identified as a possible match for the program and tailor the proposal for each one accordingly. It is true that most funders want the same basic information. It is also true that they request it in different formats, which will require reordering sections, cutting and pasting, and possibly relabeling some sections (for instance, the problem statement may become the need statement). Occasionally, additional material may need to be added or some material deleted from the original version. When you tailor the proposal for each funder, you enable each proposal reviewer to see that the proposal is responding to the grantmaker's concerns.

- *Plan ahead.* The grantseeking process operates within a three-to-six-month window on average, and each foundation operates on its own schedule. From the time a proposal is submitted to the time a potential funder responds will be, on average, six months, and many funders have specific deadlines for receiving proposals. Develop a calendar that lists all foundation and corporation prospects and their deadlines. Also maintain a list of each funder's priorities that seem applicable to the organization's desired program, and then be sure to spell out the parts of the organization's program that fit those priorities. This calendar will help you stay organized and on track as you juggle numerous deadline dates and priority areas.

Step 1
Developing the Proposal Idea

TIME TO TAKE THE FIRST STEP. This section is dedicated to zeroing in on some key questions to help develop the proposal idea. Before the proposal writing process can begin, you must first determine which organizational programs are the most "fundable." That is, which programs have the best chance to garner the most interest from grantmakers?

Many funders indicate a preference for investing in new and expanding programs over general operating support or program continuation. Thorough research of prospective funders is critical so that grantseekers understand each funder's programmatic priorities, geographic focus, and issue areas. Funders might also have an interest in a special project, a capacity-building idea, a set of technology improvements, or building up specific capacities within organizations. This workbook focuses on a general operating support request as the model for developing a proposal.

To start developing a proposal idea, begin with the end in mind. Use the proposal included in this workbook as an example (see Resource A). Alyson Eats is an organization that has identified and is successfully meeting an unmet need in a well-defined community. As an already existing organization, rather than a start-up nonprofit, Alyson Eats is clear on its issue focus, the community it serves, its goals and objectives, and its strategies for success. Additionally, the organization wants to pilot a program targeting a specific demographic within its current community. In the case of Alyson Eats, the executive director will drive the development of the organization's annual operating plan, inclusive of the concept for a pilot program targeting teens, and will involve other staff, clients, and volunteers as appropriate. The annual operating plan for the organization will serve as the basis of the entire proposal.

The importance of having the right people at the table when the proposal plan is developed cannot be overstated. Nonprofit organizations sometimes make the serious mistake of securing funding for a program that they do not have the ability to implement or – worse yet – a program that does not meet the identified needs because it was developed without the appropriate staff people involved.

When preparing a proposal, most grantwriters start with the planning sections (problem statement, goals and objectives, strategies, evaluation, program sustainability, and budget) because these sections form the core of the proposal. Following that, they craft the organizational background section, finishing with the proposal summary and the cover letter. This workbook follows that format, keeping in mind that most foundation proposals are now submitted via online portal and with limited space. The limited space on portals means being even more succinct with grant proposal copy. Every word, space, and punctuation mark counts. (Please refer to the Helpful Hint provided in the section titled How to Use This Workbook in the frontmatter.)

The planning sections of the proposal deserve careful attention; without a clearly articulated plan, it is nearly impossible to get funding. Writing a clear, goal-oriented, thoughtful proposal is crucial. If a grantseeker can't explain who they serve, what they want to do, why they're doing it, and how they're going to do it (and measure their success in doing so), foundation staff will not have what they need to (1) understand the request and why it is worthwhile, and (2) advocate on the organization's behalf.

A general guideline is that nonprofits should expect to focus approximately 70 percent of their time on program planning (problem statement, goals and objectives, strategies, evaluation, and budget); the other 30 percent can be dedicated to crafting the organizational background statement, proposal summary, and proposal submission. Remember: submitting via an online portal is going to take some time, which needs to be factored into the overall timeline.

A good guideline to keep in mind is this: the tighter an organization's plan (annual operating or programmatic), the easier the proposal will be to write. Enter this process knowing that even with program plan in hand, it will be necessary to fine-tune the plan as the proposal is being developed. This should also be built into the timeline.

Reality Check

Pay attention to the fit. When doing prospect research, grantseekers will come across various funding opportunities, including special initiatives and grants for specific programs within defined areas of interest. These opportunities might be tempting, but organizations should take care in evaluating these opportunities against their organization's mission, goals, and objectives. Is there *really* a fit? Or is the organization "growing another foot" to "fit the shoe" the funder is presenting? Grantseekers should always keep the mission, goals, and objectives of their organization at the forefront of every funding opportunity.

Helpful Hint

LOGIC MODEL

What exactly is a logic model? It is a valuable tool that provides a visual illustration of the flow of activities that will produce the desired results by the organization or program. Even the most basic logic model can prove useful in organizing the planning and analysis of an organization or programmatic design for outcomes-based evaluations. For the purpose of developing grant proposals, a logic model can be helpful in visually describing the organization and/or its programs. Some foundations require a logic model, including the W.K. Kellogg Foundation, which offers a useful Logic Model Development Guide (https://bit.ly/1HgeuAH).

To begin developing the proposal idea, complete Worksheet 1.1. The more thorough the answers, the more helpful the worksheet. After completing the worksheet, use those answers to identify one idea to focus on as you develop a grant proposal using the exercises in this workbook. To check the merit of the idea identified, answer the Proposal Development Review Questions at the end of this chapter, then follow Steps 2 through 12 to create a well-planned, winning grant. Throughout the steps, this workbook will refer you to the accompanying website for worksheet examples and templates.

WORKSHEET 1.1:
Proposal Idea Questionnaire

On the Web

1. What new projects are you planning for the next two to three years?

   Project A:

   Project B:

   Project C:

   Project D:

2. Which of these projects are most compatible with your organization's current mission and purpose, and in what way?

Project	Compatibility
A	
B	
C	
D	

3. What is unique about your organization's project?

Project	Uniqueness
A	
B	
C	
D	

WORKSHEET 1.1:
Proposal Idea Questionnaire (Continued)

4. What other organizations are doing this project? Is there duplication of effort? Is there potential for collaboration?

Duplicate Project (with whom)   Possible Collaboration Project (with whom)

A

B

C

D

5. What community need does each of your organization's projects address?

Project   Need Addressed

A

B

C

D

6. What members of your community—including civic leaders, political figures, the media, your organization's clients or constituents, and other nonprofits—support each project?

Project   Supporters

A

B

C

D

WORKSHEET 1.1:
Proposal Idea Questionnaire (Continued)

7. Does your organization currently have the expertise to undertake each project? If new staff is necessary, can the organization manage growth in infrastructure (HR, technology, supervisory oversight, and so forth) effectively? (Check each category that applies to each project.)

Project	Expertise	HR	Technology	Other (specify)
A				
B				
C				
D				

8. Is there internal (board and staff) support for the project? External support (community leaders, clients, neighbors, and so forth)? (Check the category that applies to each project and specify the type of support.)

Project	Internal Support (specify)	External Support (specify)
A		
B		
C		
D		

Public Funders

Before you begin developing a proposal concept for a public funding application, be sure to read through all grant requirements, funding restrictions, and regulations that are available. Pay particular attention to eligibility requirements. You don't want to waste time on an application only to find out your organization or program is not eligible for the funding. Another tip for developing public funding proposals is that it is often possible to find examples of proposals that have been funded under previous solicitations. Looking through successful proposals may help you as you develop your own concept!

Proposal Development Review Questions

To test whether your proposal idea has merit, answer the following six questions.

1. What community need does the organization's program or service address? The answer to this question will become the framework for the proposal's need statement.

2. What would an improved community situation look like? This answer will become the basis of the proposal's goals and objectives.

3. What can the organization do to improve the situation? This answer will become the basis of the proposal's strategies.

4. How will the organization know if its program or service has succeeded? This answer will become the basis of the proposal's evaluation component.

5. How much will the organization's program or service cost and what other sources of support (revenue and in-kind support) will it have? This answer will become the basis of the proposal's budget.

6. How will the organization's program or service be funded in the future? This answer will become the basis of the proposal's sustainability component.

Step 2
Developing Relationships with Funders

WE HAVE ALL HEARD THE ADAGES: "fundraising is about relationships" or "people give to people who work at organizations." The hard truth for grantwriters is that we can write a compelling, well-conceived, and beautifully written proposal and submit it on time with all the required attachments, only to receive a message of rejection weeks or months later. Often that message will include little more than a "thank you for applying," and no insight into why our project failed to receive funding. It can be a frustrating process.

In this chapter, we look at ways to identify, research, and develop relationships with funders to increase the likelihood that our proposals result in positive funding decisions.

Prospect Research

There are multiple ways to identify and research prospective funders. Appendix B in the Resource section and on the *Winning Grants Step by Step, Fifth Edition* website provides detailed information and tips on how to conduct prospect research to identify possible funders. A short summary of some of the methods available to grantseekers includes:

- Free online resources such a grant alerts from a city or state office that compiles open grant opportunities.

- Paid online subscription services such as the Foundation Directory Online.

- Researching the funders of peer organizations, which may be available in their annual reports, 990's, or GuideStar profiles.

- Professional prospect researchers who can provide detailed profiles of potential funders.

- Free community-based research centers and libraries, including The Foundation Center.

- Other helpful places to look for information about funders include industry publications (e.g., *The Chronicle of Philanthropy*, *Inside Philanthropy*, and others).

Once you have identified a prospective funder, you will want to gather as much information as possible about the grantmaker's funding interests, grantmaking process, board and staff members, and other details that will help in developing the right approach. A grantmaker's website is the first place to start – many, but not all, websites contain direct links to grant guidelines, supporting materials, lists of past grantees, funding restrictions, application deadlines, and the preferred method of approach. Foundations, like all 501(c)(3) organizations, are required by law to provide access to their Internal Revenue Service Form 990, which is their annual tax return. Many may have a link to this document on their websites, or the 990s can be located by visiting GuideStar (www.guidestar.org) or the Foundation Center (www.foundationcenter.org).

Some funders may require additional sleuthing on the part of the grantseeker to glean whether there is truly a match. Foundations that have small or part-time staffs, or those that only give to preselected organizations, tend to have less information available online.

Another helpful step before making an initial approach to a funder is to speak with other grantees about their experience in developing a relationship with the funder. Finally, you will want to look for any existing relationships between your organization and the funder – does a member of your board know anyone on the board or staff of the foundation? Does it make sense for the board member to make an introduction? Did the funder provide support to your organization in the past? If so, for what program?

It is helpful to develop a tool to track prospects. Many organizations use databases or Customer Relationship Management (CRM) software – such as SalesForce, DonorPerfect, Raiser's Edge, or Salsa – to manage this process. But for organizations managing a small number of prospects, a simple system can be managed in a spreadsheet that might look something like this:

Name of Funder	Contact Person	Funding Areas and Grant Range	Relationships	Action Items	Due Date
Future Foundation	Lisa Bryant, Program Officer	After-school programs for middle school youth; Hunger and food security $10,000—$50,000	Board member Alex Smith knows Lisa Bryant personally	Letter of Inquiry due	8/1/2019

You now have a fuller picture of the funder's interests, grantmaking process, and any past support of your organization – and you are ready to start the process of developing the relationship.

Developing the Relationship

After establishing that there is a good fit between your organization and the funder, relationship building becomes a continuous process that begins before a single word of a proposal is written. Strategic communication with funders should continue before, during, and even after the funding relationship has ended.

Here are a few concrete ways to approach a funder to open the door to relationship building. These are discussed more fully in the following subsections.

- Send the funder a brief email inquiry, unless the foundation's website discourages or prohibits email outreach.

- Call the foundation and request to speak with someone regarding your proposal idea, unless the foundation's website discourages or prohibits phone calls.

- Send a brief (no longer than two pages unless the funder expresses the need for more detail) letter of inquiry (LOI) to the funder. Be sure to follow the funder's guidelines for LOIs.

- Invite the funder to your organization for an event that demonstrates your organization's programs and effectiveness.

- Although grant guidelines may determine an organization's initial approach, grantseekers may have a connection to the funder, such as a board member who can potentially open a door on behalf of the organization for an initial meeting or phone conversation.

Reality Check

Be strategic and err on the side of restraint when using a contact to open a door with a funder. Few things are worse than dealing with a program officer who feels pushed into a meeting. Grantseekers always want an invitation, rather than a meeting based on obligation. Think "soft touch" rather than "heavy hand."

Once a relationship exists, staying on a funder's radar screen is imperative and can be accomplished, if permitted by the funder, outside of their required reporting structures. These "touches" may spark the funder's interest in other compelling ideas and programs that the organization has developed.

Sending Email Inquiries to Funders

Many funders offer grantseekers the option of contacting them via email with questions and funding inquiries. Some grantmakers even provide direct email access to their program officers from their websites; others may have an "info@" email that is routed to the appropriate staff person after review. In either case, email is a valuable tool for stimulating further, more meaningful, contact because it provides an opportunity for a brief introduction of a staff person, the organization represented, and the program needing funding. At the same time, it gives program officers the time they need to review the information and potentially respond. The key is to keep it brief! Resist the urge to write a mini-proposal in the email. In the email, grantseekers can also request an in-person meeting or time for a phone conversation, which then provides the funder with options for responding to the communication.

Contacting a Funder by Telephone

Before calling a funder to pitch an idea, be prepared. The person you speak with may have only a short time for a conversation, so preparation is essential. Be ready to provide the highlights of your organization's program within a 10- to 15-minute conversation. This time frame includes the time it may take for the person to ask for clarification of any points. Grantseekers should remember that they are not selling their organization's program to a funder; rather, they are attempting to make a connection between the program and the funding institution's interest areas. To build a long-term relationship with the funder and with this particular representative, careful and engaged listening to the funder's interests and providing information the funder wants is extremely important.

In listening to the funder's interests, you might discover – sometimes very early in the conversation – that in fact there is not a match between your organization's program and the funder's current funding priorities; that is why grantseekers should have one or two other program ideas in mind to present as a backup. Do not waste this opportunity with the funder; be fully prepared with information on identified unmet needs that may fit into the funder's interest areas. **Finally, make sure to reiterate any follow-up steps resulting from the call and to send a quick thank-you email for the program officer's time.**

Funder Meetings

In an ideal world, grantseekers would get the opportunity to meet face-to-face with a funder before they submit a proposal – either at the funder's office or, even better, at the grantseeker's organization. Such meetings allow the development of a personal relationship and, in the case of a site visit, for the funder to see an organization or program in action. Unfortunately, pre-proposal funder meetings are often hard to arrange because funders simply cannot accommodate every nonprofit's request for them. Also, some funders are leery of these meetings because they do not want to raise unrealistic funding expectations. Managing grantseeker expectations is of the utmost importance to the majority of funders: they want to encourage the submission of solid proposals for programs meeting their interest areas, but at the same time, they do not want to raise false hopes. Remember, every foundation and corporate grantmaker has a limited amount of funding available for grants every year. That said, if an organization has a contact that already has a strong relationship with a funder, this individual may be able to help broker a meeting; but understand that any early meeting secured with the grantmaker will be very preliminary and in no way ensures that the grantseeker will receive funds from this source.

If an in-person meeting is scheduled, grantseekers should have materials available that best describe the organization and the proposed program. In the meeting, the grantseeker should attempt to cover the following topics:

- Credibility of the organization

- Need for the proposed project

- Program description

- Community interest in the program

- Proposed outcomes

- Ability to measure success

- Costs and projected revenue sources

- Why this funder's interests may be met by investing in the program

Time with a program officer is likely to be short, so organizations should be prepared to hit the highlights. Listen carefully to the funder's questions and any concerns expressed, and make sure questions are answered fully and truthfully. These questions and concerns should also be addressed again in the proposal that will be submitted following the meeting, provided there is a good fit.

Here are some additional steps to take to develop good relationships with funders to whom the grantseeker has spoken:

- Add the program officer to the organization's mailing list or listserv.

- Personally forward your organization's newsletter, and go the extra distance by including a personal note.

- Send brief (one- to two-page) progress reports on the successes of the organization's work – activities that the program officer has not funded but that colleagues at other funding institutions may have funded.

- Invite the program officer to organization events with personal notes – even if she cannot come, she will remember the contact.

- Contact the program officer occasionally by telephone or email with brief messages and updates. Include quotes or even notes from program constituents.

Writing a Letter of Inquiry

A *letter of inquiry* (sometimes called letter of intent – the shorthand for both is LOI) can be the first step in a funder's grantmaking process. You may be asked to submit an LOI after engaging in the relationship building strategies described above. Or you may be submitting an LOI "cold" – with no prior contact – in hopes that it will be well-received by the funder and result in a phone conversation, meeting, or invitation to submit a full proposal.

An LOI provides the funder with a "sneak peek" at the organization, target audience, and prospective program, without requiring the grantseeker to develop a full proposal at this early stage. After the funder has reviewed the information presented in the LOI, the organization may or may not be invited to submit a full proposal. Even though an LOI is a preliminary step, it should be treated as a vital part of relationship building. It is an integral early interaction of what grantseekers hope will be many interactions with the funder. The first step is to check to see whether the funder has specific LOI guidelines. If it does not, the following guidelines cover what information to include, as a general rule:

- The organization's mission, history, accomplishments, related programs

- The need the organization or program meets and who it serves

- The outcomes expected from the organization's project

- General details of how the organization will conduct the project

- How the project or organization aligns with the funder's priorities

- Organizational or project budget and funding need

- Basic attachments may be required during the LOI stage, including organizational budget and IRS determination letter. Be sure to check the requirements.

The sample LOI included in this step presents Alyson Eats to a prospective funder. This is the letter that Alyson Eats' executive director would submit if an LOI was invited by the funder or if the funder accepted unsolicited submissions.

Sample Letter of Inquiry

Date
Ms. Wendy Wonder
President
Future Foundation
0000 Clinton Avenue, Suite 2330
Anytown, Any State 02009

Dear Ms. Wonder:

As follow-up to my recent conversation with Lisa Bryant, I am pleased to submit this Letter of Inquiry for Alyson Eats for your consideration. We are respectfully requesting a general support grant of $50,000 for our comprehensive programs to address hunger and food insecurity in some of our community's most underserved areas.

Since 2004, Alyson Eats has sought to ease the suffering of some of the approximately 130,000 residents of Alyson who are experiencing or at risk for hunger. Our objective over the coming year is to provide more than 200,000 nutritious meals to hungry children and adults on Alyson's south side.

Alyson Eats will engage our nine staff members (five are part-time), our 50 regular volunteers, and our corporate and other institutional partners across the city to conduct three proven programs to address hunger: our food pantry and distribution service, which will distribute approximately 9,000 boxes of food this year; a summer-time program that will provide meals to about 1,000 children who normally get free lunch at school; and an outreach program to recruit and engage donors of food and funds, as well as volunteers, with a goal this year of recruiting 15 new volunteers and generating 4,500 additional hours of volunteer engagement. We will also pilot a new program to equip teenagers with the skills to eat healthfully and affordably for life, beginning with a class of 30 young people. The Fiscal Year 2020 budget of Alyson Eats is $1,352,016. We have secured commitments for about 85 percent of our budget.

Thank you for inviting Alyson Eats to submit this Letter of Inquiry. Because of our shared commitment to building a better future for families struggling with poverty in our state, we hope that the Future Foundation will invite a full proposal for $50,000 in general operating support for the one-year period beginning January 1. If you have any questions, please feel free to call me at (111) 111–1111.

Sincerely,
Shawna Jones
Executive Director

Now that a sample LOI has been presented and reviewed, take the time to answer the questions in Worksheet 2.1. This exercise will help in developing a strong letter of inquiry for funders. If you cannot clearly and succinctly answer the questions, that probably means you need to gather more information before you can effectively complete an LOI.

WORKSHEET 2.1:
Letter of Inquiry Questionnaire

1. What is the purpose of this letter of inquiry? To whom is it being sent, and what is the connection?

2. Is the name of the program and amount of the request clearly stated in the first paragraph?

3. What year was the organization founded? What is the mission of the organization?

4. What are the long-term goals for the organization? What programs does the organization conduct that support these goals?

5. What is the need in the community that you seek funding to address? What population and or geographic areas does the program serve?

6. Is the need the proposed program intends to meet clear? Are some preliminary data included to support the need for the proposed program?

7. What does the organization propose to do about this need and what success has it had in the past?

8. What outcomes does the organization and/or its program(s) anticipate reaching over the next year?

9. Is program implementation briefly described?

10. Is the "fit" or natural connection between the organization's program and the funder's priority areas, as identified in their guidelines, included?

11. What is the total cost of the proposed idea for the requested year, or what is the cost to expand the current program? (Or multiple years if you plan to request multiple-year funding?) If there is some funding already committed to the project, is it mentioned?

12. How much is being requested from the funder, for what time period, and how will it be used?

13. Is the program's contact person clearly identified, including all contact information?

Reality Check: Submitting LOIs

Most funders have online portals through which you can submit your LOI, and/or they accept them by email. If the funder has an online portal, be sure to register your organization well in advance of the LOI deadline to avoid any technical issues. Follow the funder's guidelines on how to submit, paying attention to:

- LOI deadlines – including the time of day. Some funders close their portals at 5 p.m. while others close at 11:59 p.m. on the deadline day.
- LOI format – including character and page length limitations.
- LOI required attachments – which will usually need to be saved in PDF format and uploaded.

Public Funders

Building relationships with public funders can be a very different process from the one described for foundations and corporate funders. The nature of the public funding process requires government entities and employees to maintain impartial positions toward grantseekers and ensure that all applicants for public funding have access to the same information. For this reason, information about public funding and opportunities to engage with government officials are generally open to all and may include:

- **Notice of Funding Availability (NOFA):** a notice published describing funding that may become or is available on a competitive basis, how much funding is available, the goals of the funding program, where an application may be found and submitted, due dates, eligible applicants, and other information. NOFAs are often published well in advance of the actual Request for Applications.

- **Request for Applications (RFA):** The RFA is the solicitation notice in which the funding agency announces that grant funding is available, and provides information including purpose and source of funds; expected grant award amount; award period; eligibility; application content and attachments required; budget requirements; deadlines for applications; application submission requirements; process for how applications will be reviewed; dates and requirements for prebid conferences; and contact persons within the agency.

- **Prebid Conference or Webinar:** Once the RFA has been issued, many public funders will hold prebid conferences or webinars. These meetings are designed to clarify any questions that applicants may have with the solicitation documents and requirements. Be sure to read the NOFA and RFA carefully to see if attendance at one of these sessions is a requirement for submitting an application or is recommended but not required. Even if it is not required, attendance at the sessions is a great way to connect with the funding agency, get insight into the application process, and check out the competition!

- **General Information Sessions:** Sometimes, public funding agencies will hold general information sessions not tied to a funding opportunity. These are good opportunities to build relationships and understand the priorities of the funder.

Although public funding agencies follow different rules and regulations than foundation and corporations, the most savvy government grantseekers develop the visibility of their organizations with public funders long before a funding application announcement is ever made. They are active members of their communities and have allies for their work across sectors – including other nonprofit organizations, faith-based organizations, schools and institutions of higher education, elected officials, and more.

Developing relationships with funders of all kinds is such an important step in the process of winning grants that the value of doing it well cannot be emphasized enough. Now that you have explored strategies for developing funder relationships, it's time to craft the problem statement for your grant proposal in Step 3.

Step 3
Writing a Compelling Problem Statement

THIS STEP HIGHLIGHTS THE KEY ELEMENTS of a *problem statement* (which some grantmakers might call a statement of need or needs statement), including the four requirements for it to be successful. The section also offers a worksheet and sample to serve as guides to preparing a problem statement for a proposal.

Purpose of the Problem Statement

An organization's problem statement should answer the question, "What is the problem to be addressed?" Therefore this is a good place to begin writing a proposal. A problem statement sets the framework for the entire proposal, as it describes a critical condition or a social need affecting certain people or things in a specific place at a specific time.

The problem statement is fundamental to a proposal because funders must agree with the grantseeker that their program addresses an important community problem. Bolstered by accurate data (quantitative statistics) combined with the right selection of stories that provide a more personal illustration of the need (qualitative data), a compelling problem statement is often the first component that motivates a funder to give serious consideration to a nonprofit's request. In addition, the unmet need – and an organization's ability to address it – gives grantmakers an opportunity to realize their own goals and advance their own mission.

A solid and well-supported problem statement is the key that unlocks the door, moving a proposal that much closer to funding consideration.

Content of the Problem Statement

Here are some basic rules to follow when developing the proposal's problem statement:

- The need being addressed in the statement should have a clear relationship to your organization's mission and purpose.

- The problem statement should focus squarely on those communities the organization serves and their needs, rather than the organization's needs – unless the organization is seeking a capacity-building grant.

- Any assertions about the problem should be supported with evidence (statistical facts, expert views, trends found in the experience of doing the work, and so on).

- The organization must be able to connect – and substantiate – the need described in the proposal with the organization's ability to respond to that need.

- The problem statement must be easily digestible. Avoid using jargon, and do not make the reader have to work to understand the point. Graphs and charts with data to support the case can be good additions, as they present the data in a visual way.

The problem being addressed by the organization may be specific to its geographical area or it may be found in many communities. It may be nationwide or worldwide. Do not overpromise: define the piece of the problem that your organization can address.

If the problem exceeds the boundaries of the organization or proposed program, consider positioning the program as a potential model for other nonprofits in other locations. This enables the organization to broaden the pool of potential funders to include those concerned with the problem in other geographical areas. Begin by conducting research to discover whether other organizations in the service area have – or are developing – similar programs to address the same problem. If so, consider exploring a collaborative program that would leverage and expand the reach of each organization's program plans and grant funds. Of course, consider these options only if they actually advance the organization's goals, not simply to attract a funder.

If the organization decides to take either the model or collaborative approach, highlight this fact in the problem statement; the organization is addressing the need on a larger level through the development of a program that can be a model for others, or through leveraging its efforts with another organization (or more than one) so it can expand the reach and impact of its program.

Reality Check

Keep in mind that conducting a program as a replicable model or a collaboration will require different and possibly greater resources and effort than it would take to conduct the program itself. For instance, if an organization positions its program as a model for other nonprofits to replicate, it must document the program and its impacts much more thoroughly than it might otherwise. It must produce a report or training curriculum or some kind of mechanism that will enable others to replicate the program. It must develop a dissemination plan and conduct outreach to let others know about the program and how to replicate it. The additional cost and work are among the reasons why proposing a model program or collaboration should not be undertaken solely as a fundraising tactic, but only if such an approach will serve the organization's mission and constituency.

Often arts organizations struggle with the problem statement section, owing to a perception that the arts do not meet a compelling community need. However, arts organizations should be encouraged, as they do meet important needs. Without these nonprofits, certain cultures and traditions would be lost, lives would not be enriched, and young people would not learn new and different ways of thinking or of expressing themselves.

The same holds true for social justice organizations that may struggle with how to quantify social change. Over the last few years, there has been more research in this area, and the Resource section (Resource C) offers some guidance on how best to frame social justice goals.

For general support grants, writing a problem statement may seem challenging because the proposal addresses the general work of the organization. Use the nonprofit's mission and purpose as a guide, and focus on describing the problems that the organization addresses.

Definition

Collaboration: Projects and programs undertaken by a partnership of multiple nonprofit organizations because the scope or complexity of the project will benefit from each organization's particular expertise or provided services, or will enable more effective and efficient delivery of the program or services than individual organizations working alone or separately. It includes:

- Jointly developing and agreeing upon a set of common goals and direction.
- Sharing the risks and responsibility for obtaining those goals.
- Working together to achieve those goals, using the expertise and resources of each collaborator.
- Jointly developed structure.[1]

Tips for Writing the Problem Statement

The problem statement should be concise. Many foundations require organizations to submit grant proposals through online portals that limit the available space to a specific number of words or even characters. (See the section on How to Use This Workbook for tips on how to write concisely.) Even if this is not the case, foundation guidelines often limit proposals to eight to 10 pages in total; corporate guidelines typically limit proposals to even fewer pages. The problem statement should take up only one or two of those pages, so the organization can use the majority of the space to write about how they will address the problem.

In stating the problem, use hard statistics from reputable sources and steer clear of assumptions and undocumented assertions masquerading as legitimate facts.

- *Use statistics that are clear and that document the current unmet need or problem.* If talking about a particular community within a city, offer one or two data points about the city, then zero in on the data specific to that community.

- *Use comparative statistics and research where appropriate.* Using data from a community that did something very similar to what you want to do and citing the benefits that the community derived from the project can make a strong case for your nonprofit to do the same.

- *Quote authorities who have spoken on the topic.* Be sure to cite the person who made each statement and the source where it was found, and if appropriate, provide backup information that substantiates that this person is indeed an authority on the subject matter.

- *Make sure all data collection is well documented.* When researching online, make sure that the websites being referenced are reputable and the links are both accurate and current; then cite the sources.

- *Use compelling stories of people as examples.* This is very effective, but only when balanced against hard data. Keep in mind that foundations vary in what they seek in terms of the right mix of vignettes and numbers. Follow their guidelines.

- *Give a clear sense of the urgency of the request.* Funders need to understand why the funding is important now.

Take a look at the following sample problem statement from the Alyson Eats program. (This statement is very brief; others can be longer, if the foundation guidelines allow it.) Then, using the proposal idea identified and developed in Step One, answer the questions on Worksheet 3.1A, as this will assist in defining the need the organization is addressing. (Worksheet 3.1B shows how Alyson Eats would fill out the worksheet.) After reviewing the sample problem statement and completing the worksheet questionnaire, write the organization's problem statement based on the information developed. Next, answer the Problem Statement Review Questions listed at the end of this step to make sure the statement is written well. Rewrite the problem statement until all the review questions are satisfactorily addressed.

Helpful Hint

PROBLEM STATEMENTS FOR PUBLIC FUNDING

In the case of public funding, government entities are often very specific about the needs that they expect to be addressed by applicants, and grantseekers must pay close attention to the language used in Requests for Applications. For example, public funders may issue exact requirements for the population to be served (e.g., a specific demographic group), the geographic area(s) to be targeted, or the specific community need to be met.

Some other important tips for writing needs statements (or problem statements) for public funding:

- Use the most up-to-date government statistics available to document need. Some public funders specify the source of data – such as the FBI Uniform Crime Report or U.S. Census data – that must be presented in the need statement.

- Mirror the language used by the grantmaking agency in describing the target population, area to be served, and so forth.

- Participant stories and anecdotes often work well in foundation and corporate proposals but may not be right for many public funding applications. Be thoughtful about how you use anecdotal information in the needs statement.

- Public funding applications are usually scored on a point system. Pay attention to points given for specific areas of need and be sure to specially address those that can be awarded the highest points.

- Above all else, follow the RFA instructions to the letter so that you don't lose points or become disqualified on a technicality.

Sample Problem Statement

Approximately 130,000 residents of Alyson, most of them living on the city's south side, are at risk for hunger. On the south side, most children qualify for free lunch at school (76%). Adults sometimes skip meals because there is not enough food in the home (39%), and many parents worry at the beginning of the month how they will feed their children by the end of the month (45%), as a survey conducted last year by the Alyson City Council revealed. The summer months are particularly difficult because schools, and school lunch programs, are closed.

Convenience stores, take-out places, and fast-food restaurants abound on the south side, and many families must make do with the food they offer. Fresh, nutritious food is not only more expensive than less-nutritious food ($1.50 a day costlier, according to researchers at the Harvard School of Public Health), but also geographically out of reach for most residents of the south side, a large proportion of whom do not own cars. Only one-third of the neighborhoods in the south side are within reasonable distance – less than three miles – of a full-service grocery store via public transit. As a result, many south-side children grow up rarely having been in a supermarket, and with no opportunity to learn the consumer skills that can enable them to choose and afford healthful food throughout their lives.

We know that hunger is not merely the lack of food; it is the lack of access to resources, economic opportunity and social mobility – in other words, poverty. While Alyson Eats supports and partners with organizations that fight the root causes of poverty, including several grantees of the Future Foundation, our goal is more immediate: to reduce the suffering of those who are hungry. To this end we conduct a number of programs that serve and involve the low-income residents of Alyson's south side.

WORKSHEET 3.1A:
Statement of Problem Questionnaire

Who? Where? When?	What? Why?	Evidence of Problem	Impact If Problems Resolved?
Who is in need (people, animals, land, and so forth)?	What is the problem? (Get specific)	What evidence do you have to support your claim?	What will occur if the needs are met? What will be different—and how?
Where are they? (General: city/state; and specific: neighborhood, geography)	Why does this problem exist?		How is the problem linked to your organization?
When is the problem evident?			

On the Web

WORKSHEET 3.1B:
Statement of Problem Questionnaire, filled out by Alyson Eats

Who? Where? When?	What? Why?	Evidence of Problem	Impact If Problems Resolved?
Who is in need (people, animals, land, and so forth)? About 130,000 people	What is the problem? (Get specific) Approximately 13% of Alyson's population lives in hunger or at risk of hunger (food insecure)	What evidence do you have to support your claim? Data from U.S. Census bureau, recent survey by Alyson city council, direct observation	What will occur if the needs are met? What will be different – and how? Adults and children are healthier when they are not hungry, students learn better, parents experience less stress.
Where are they? (General: city/state; and specific: neighborhood, geography) Living on the south side of the city of Alyson	Why does this problem exist? Long-term disinvestment in the primarily people-of-color neighborhoods on the city's south side		How is the problem linked to your organization? The mission of Alyson Eats is to reduce the suffering of hunger on the city's south side. We can't solve the problem but can ease it considerably for the thousands of families we serve.
When is the problem evident? The problem is ongoing, but exacerbated in the summer when children are not provided school lunches			

Problem Statement Review Questions

Once a problem statement is completed, answer the following six questions to see whether the statement hits the mark:

1. Is the problem statement focused on those who will be served by the program (and not on your organization)?

2. Does the problem statement directly connect to the organization's mission statement?

3. Does the statement explain how the organization, given its size and resources, can address the problem in a meaningful way?

4. Is the problem statement adequately supported by solid and reputable quantitative and qualitative data on the nature, size, and scope of the need to be addressed?

5. Is it sweet and simple (remember KISS from a previous chapter)?

6. Is the problem statement persuasive without being wordy?

Reality Check

Avoid the trap of circular reasoning, which commonly occurs in problem statements. To use the Foundation Center's definition, circular reasoning occurs when "you present the absence of your solution as the actual problem. Then your solution is offered as the way to solve the problem." For example, "The problem is that our community has no food program for children during the summer. Conducting a summer food program for children will solve the problem."

This statement does not communicate a problem: communities across the country thrive with no summer food program for children. However, if the proposal establishes that such a program would address certain challenges the community is facing and, if the proposed program is new, cites a similar community where a summer food program has had a positive impact in ways that are documented, it could build a compelling argument that would provide the context for the problem statement. In the sample proposal, the organization has conducted the program for years, and has its own data to demonstrate the community's need and the program's impact.

The program's need is now established. Developing the program's goals and objectives is next, which is Step 4.

Note

1. Definition courtesy of the Greater Green Bay Community Foundation, https://www.ggbcf.org/-Grant-Scholarship-Seekers/Grants-Process/Definition-of-Collaboration.

Step 4
Defining Clear Goals and Objectives

IN THIS STEP GRANTSEEKERS LEARN the concept of writing clear goals and objectives – and the important differences between those two terms. Using the website and following the examples, grantseekers construct goals and a set of objectives for their own proposals.

Purpose of the Goals and Objectives Components: The "So What?" Factor

Once an organization has articulated (in the problem or need statement) the problem to be addressed, the next step is to develop solid goals that define what the organization intends to accomplish through its program, and establish measurable objectives that will indicate the organization's progress toward its goals. The goals and objectives will allow the organization and its funders to know whether the program is successful at the conclusion of the grant. Poorly defined goals and objectives, or goals without objectives, push projects into missed milestones, overworked staff, unhappy clients, and disillusioned funders. Goals and objectives should be clear statements of purpose that define the end result of the project.[1]

Definition of Goals and Objectives

Some terms can be confusing, especially if the assumption is made that everyone understands what they mean. So it's important to keep in mind that *goals* are what the program aspires to achieve, and *objectives* "should clarify what changes you expect to see as a result of your work."[2] Don't confuse the organization's *mission*, which is its ongoing reason for existence, with the organization's *goals*, which are more narrowly focused on an organization's programs and projects, and which might change from year to year.

Many foundations ask grantseekers to break down their objectives into smaller pieces, such as activities and outcomes, and some grantmakers use their own particular definitions. For this reason, it is essential to review each foundation's guidelines and follow their instructions. Other terms some grantmakers might use under the general umbrella of goals and objectives include:

Activities: the work that the organization will undertake in order to achieve its goals.

Outcomes (sometimes used interchangeably with *objectives*; some foundations call these *accomplishments*): what will have changed as the result of the organization's work during the course of this grant.

Outputs: materials or other products the grantseeker's program will produce, such as a training video.

Measures of success (sometimes called *benchmarks*): how the organization will know it has achieved its objectives.

Some foundations ask grantseekers to articulate what they expect to achieve within different timeframes. For instance, some grantmakers ask for short- and long-term objectives – and they may define these terms in their own way. To one foundation, a short-term objective may mean what the grantseeker can achieve within the grant period, while another foundation may define short-term as over the next three years. These definitions will be spelled out in the foundation's guidelines.

An organization may have more than one goal, and each goal may have more than one objective. In the sample proposal, for example, the organization as a whole has one goal and one objective. However, the organization conducts four programs, each of which has its own goal and objective. These four program objectives add up to the organizational objective. A smaller program may have only one goal and two or three objectives. What is important is that both the goals and the objectives are directly tied to the problem statement (Step 3).

Goal: The "thing(s) you're attempting to accomplish," which "show the funder that you have a vision for solving the problem."[3] Grantseekers might have goals for their organization as a whole, and/or for their programs. A good approach is to make sure a goal is SMART: Specific, Measurable, Achievable, Relevant and Time-bound. (Variations of the SMART formula abound: for instance, replacing Achievable with Ambitious, or Relevant with Realistic. It's a tool – use the SMART definitions that work best for the project at hand.)

Example: (Organizational goal) Reduce hunger in the city of Alyson.

(Program goal – Every Youngster Eats) Reduce the summer school-lunch gap for 1,000 children.

Objective: A "major milestone ... or benchmark on your route to reaching a goal."[4] An objective must be measurable.

Example: (Organizational objective) Provide more than 200,000 nutritious meals to children and adults in Alyson who are experiencing or are at risk for hunger.

Writing tip

When writing an objective, use verbs (action words), such as increase, decrease, reduce, improve, gain, create, provide, equip, and so on.

(Program objective – Every Youngster Eats) 1,000 children will receive lunch five days a week from June through August (12 weeks), for a total of 60,000 meals.

Everyone struggles in the beginning with the difference between goals and objectives. Use the side-by-side comparison in Table 4.1 as an aid.[5]

Outcome-Focused Objectives

It is important to ensure that a grant proposal's objectives focus on outcomes (the change) versus the process (how the change will be made). The "how" is addressed in the next step, which centers on strategies. Outcomes answer these questions: What will be different, improved, or better as the results of an organization's actions? What can be measured?

An example of an outcome objective: "1,000 children will receive lunch five days a week from June through August." There is another kind of objective, sometimes called process objectives. These focus on activities, for example, "To distribute ready-made meals to childcare centers, nonprofit day camps, and so forth, to make up for the school lunches that children rely on during the school year."

Although there is a place for process objectives (see the Reality Check later), foundations are generally more interested in outcomes – in what an organization expects to achieve. In fact, a common error grantseekers make is to confuse activities ("We will conduct a program to distribute ready-made meals") with outcomes ("1,000 children will receive lunch five days a week").

As one example of a foundation's guidelines, the Morris & Gwendolyn Cafritz Foundation in Washington, DC asks four clear and simple questions an organization should answer pertaining to the problem statement and outcomes:[6]

1. What problem/need does this project address?

Table 4.1   Goals versus Objectives

Goals	Objectives
Are broad statements	Are realistic steps to achieve the goal(s)
Provide focus, vision, and direction	Are active and use strong action verbs
Can be idealistic and do not necessarily have to be reached during the proposed grant period	Answer: What? Why? Who? How? When?
Can be nonspecific and nonmeasurable	Can be validated
	Are clear to everyone with a basic knowledge
	Are SMART:
	Specific
	Measurable
	Achievable
	Relevant
	Time-bound

Example of Strong Goals and Objectives

Goals	Objectives
All children have a playground within walking distance	Increase the access to playgrounds for children in Eastown by two playgrounds each year for the next five years.
Asthma is no longer the number one reason that children miss school	All students in grades K–3 who are diagnosed with asthma decrease their incidents of severe attacks by 15 percent in the first semester.
All adults can read confidently to their children	Eighty-five percent of first-time, new parents in the Barrisville section of Anytown can read and have child-appropriate books in their homes within a year of their first child's birth.

2. What is your organization's proposed solution to this problem/need, and how will it be implemented?

3. What evidence will prove the success of this project?

4. What results are you committed to achieving during the grant period?

Step 3 emphasized that the problem statement must focus on what the community needs, not what the organization needs; similarly, objectives should focus on what change the organization will achieve, not what the organization will do. The outcome-focused approach benefits an organization by allowing it the flexibility to adjust its strategies and activities as needed to reach its objectives – and ultimately to achieve its goals.

Definitions

1. *Goal* is what the program will achieve. Goals are visionary and may not be measurable.

2. *Objectives* are how grantseekers will know if their program is meeting its goal(s). Objectives are measurable and time-bound.

3. *Strategies* define the activities or methods needed to accomplish the objectives. Strategies are the "how to."

Because outcomes are considered powerful indicators of success, this workbook focuses more on outcome objectives rather than process objectives. A growing numbers of funders, as well as individual donors, are looking to make an impact with their grants. A grantseeker's outcome-focused objectives will help funders understand how their investment in the organization will make an impact by creating positive change.

Reality Check: Advocacy

Creating systems change, advocating for a community, group of people or position, and/or enabling community activism takes time, and the path to success is not always clear or easy to quantify. Because of the nature of this work, grantseekers may want to include process objectives as well as outcome objectives. These process objectives are the small wins that allow everyone to measure the progress in moving toward the goals.

Example for Advocacy Work

Outcome: Schools replace high-sugar snacks with nutritious snacks in vending machines on campus.

Process or small win: Have a proposition on the November ballot banning high-sugar snacks in school vending machines.

Process or small win: Collect enough signatures to be on the November ballot.

The following chart contains some questions that may help grantseekers define better outcomes.[7]

Process-Oriented Questions	Outcome-Oriented Questions
What services do you offer?	What community results do you hope to accomplish through your services?
What is it that your organization does?	What is it that your organization is striving to achieve?
What service needs does your organization or agency meet?	What change in condition or behavior are you attempting to effect in the people you serve?

Writing Outcome Objectives

Answering the following questions will help to articulate the results the organization expects to accomplish:

- Based on the problem statement, *what* is (are) the key area(s) the organization is seeking to change?

- *Who* (what segment of the population or community) will be involved in the change?

- *How* will the change be measured (an increase or improvement, or a decrease and reduction)? And by what degree (by how much)?

- *When* will this change take place? How many months or years or by what specific date?

After you have written your objectives, it is helpful to run one last test to see if the objectives are SMART:[8]

- Specific: Do they answer some or all of the five W questions about what change the organization wants to create (who, what, when, where, why)?

- Measurable: How will you know if you've met the goal? What metrics will you use? What benchmarks will serve as stepping stones to the final goal?

- Achievable: This is the reality check. Based on available resources (knowledge, funding, staffing, partners, physical space, etc.) and access to the target population, will the organization be able to make the change it envisions within the defined time? And with the resources requested? It is important to strike a balance between being overly ambitious and aiming too low.

- Relevant: Are the objectives results-oriented and rewarding to the organization, its funder(s), and, most important, the community being served?

- Time-bound: What is the deadline for reaching the change envisioned?

Reality Check

The SMART system has been in use for many years. The Management Center, which serves as a resource on effective management for social change organizations, has updated this tool with measures that are important to both foundations and grantseekers today.[9] Their "SMARTIE" system includes the classic SMART descriptions, and adds:

- **Inclusive**: Brings traditionally marginalized people – particularly those most impacted – into processes, activities, and decision/policy making in a way that shares power.

- **Equitable:** Includes an element of fairness or justice that seeks to address systemic injustice, inequity, or oppression.

  "SMARTIE goals are about including marginalized communities in a way that shares power, shrinks disparities, and leads to more equitable outcomes," The Management Center explains. This approach can be used for any kind of program, from direct service to arts organizations.

Helpful Hint

Objectives measure a change: an increase or improvement, a decrease or reduction, or the creation of something that didn't exist previously. Active phrases, like "our objective is to reduce X" are crisper than more passive phrases, such as "our objective is reducing X." As much as possible, avoid using words that end in "ing."

Public Funding: Goals and Objectives

Unlike private funders, public funders often provide specific goals and objectives they expect grantees to be able to meet, and applicants should be sure to state that they will meet those projected benchmarks in their goals and objectives. These expected goals and objectives may be tied to laws and regulations that authorize the funding opportunities. For example, many local public workforce development programs derive their funding from the multibillion-dollar, federal Workforce Innovation and Opportunity Act (WIOA). WIOA has specific performance measures related to job placement, job retention, attainment of credentials, and building relationships with employers, among others, that applicants must be prepared to address in their applications.

Public-funding applications may ask for goals and objectives to be stated in specific formats and/or to be presented in logic model format. Be sure to follow formatting directions to the letter.

As described in Step 1, a logic model is a graphic representation of the program and its outcomes. If a logic model is required, there may be a sample provided the RFA. If not, there are many free downloadable templates and sample logic models available online.

Tips for Writing Good Goals and Objectives

Do ...

- Include at least one goal for the project and one or two outcome objectives.

- Make sure that the goals and objectives tie back to the problem statement. This is critical.

- Include all relevant groups in the target population in the goal(s). When writing objectives, it's fine to specify an outcome for a particular population or community.

- Allow plenty of time to accomplish objectives. Things always take longer to implement than planned. It is better to undercommit and overperform than to overcommit and underperform.

Don't ...

- Overpromise what can be accomplished. Limit the number of goals to one to three per program and no more than three objectives per goal. An organization will need to keep track of – and report to the funder on – all the objectives tied to the goals, so keep it manageable with a small number of the most meaningful objectives.

- Confuse outcome objectives with strategies or activities. Running a food pantry is an activity. To ensure that at least 3,000 households reduce their risk of hunger over the course of the year is an outcome objective, as it describes the result expected to be achieved.

- Forget to budget for evaluation activities (Step 6) if measuring the objective(s) will have costs associated with it.

Use Worksheet 4.1A to prepare to write proposal goals and objectives by focusing on outcomes. Start by writing down the goal of the program. Then describe the objectives that tie to that goal. Use the filled-out Worksheet 4.1B as a guide. If an organization has more than one goal for its program, use a separate copy of Worksheet 4.1A for each goal. Limit the objectives to no more than three per goal.

WORKSHEET 4.1A:
Goals and Objectives Exercise

On the Web

Grantseekers should complete this worksheet for themselves. For guidance refer to Worksheet 4.1B, which contains sample goals and objectives based on the Eating Is a Right program.

GOAL:

	Objective 1	Objective 2	Objective 3
Direction of change			
Area of change			
Target population			
Degree of change			
Time frame			

Follow this standard form as objective statements are developed: To (direction of change) + (area of change) + (target population) + (degree of change) + (time frame).

WORKSHEET 4.1B:
Objectives Worksheet Completed for the Eating Is a Right Program

GOAL: To provide access to 144,000 healthful meals for individuals and families in Alyson's south side.

	Objective 1	Objective 2	Objective 3
Direction of change	Increase		
Area of change	Residents of the city of Alyson's south side		
Target population	Families who are hungry or at risk of hunger .		
Degree of change	9,000 boxes of food totaling 144,000 meals will reach at least 3,000 households		
Time frame	One full year		

When this is completed, go through the Goals and Objectives Review Questions using the same approach you used for the problem statement. Remember, the goal is to be able to answer yes to each question in the review questions.

Goals and Objectives Review Questions

1.   Are the goals stated as results? And do they relate to the problem statement?

2.   Are the outcome objectives stated as results that relate to a program goal? Are they stepping stones to achieving success (the goal)? Can everyone understand them?

3.   Can progress in meeting the objectives be measured and assessed?

4.   Do the objectives describe the population and a specific time frame for change?

The organization's problem statement is in order, and the "so what?" factor has been addressed in the program's goals and objectives. So let's move on to Step 5 where the development of the organization's strategies, or activities, will help to achieve the program's objectives, thus leading to the accomplishment of the program's goals.

Notes

1.   Rhonda Goetz, *Defining Project Goals and Objectives*, January 2010, www .projectsmart.co.uk.

2.   Walter and Evelyn Haas, Jr. Foundation Guidelines, https://www.haasjr.org/ grants/for-current-grantees/sample-objectives, accessed November 2018.

3.   Beverly A. Browning, *Grant Writing For Dummies*, 6th ed. (Hoboken, NJ: John Wiley & Sons, 2016).

4.   Ibid.

5.   Adapted from UCLA Center for Health Policy Research, Health DATA, Train the Trainer Project. *Performing a Community Assessment Curriculum*, 2004. http://healthpolicy.ucla.edu/programs/health-data/trainings/Documents/ tw_cba7.pdf.

6.   www.cafritzfoundation.org/apply/before-you-apply.

7.   Adapted from Robert A. Penna and William J. Phillips, *Outcome Frameworks* (Albany, NY: Rensselaerville Institute's Center for Outcomes, Fort Orange Press, 2004), 8.

8.   Adapted from Emily Esposito, "The Essential Gide to Writing S.M.A.R.T Goals," Smartsheet.com, https://www.smartsheet.com/blog/essential-guide-writing-smart-goals, accessed December 2018.

9.   SMARTIE Goals Worksheet, The Management Center, http://www .managementcenter.org/resources/smartie-goals-worksheet/.

Step 5
Developing the Strategies

THE STRATEGIES AN ORGANIZATION USES to reach its objectives are the focus of this step. Some funders may refer to this as a workplan. In this chapter, grantseekers look at the elements of developing the strategies component of a proposal and learn how to use a timeline to outline their plan of action. Using a worksheet and examples, organizations can write strategies that align with the objectives developed in Step 4.

Purpose of the Strategies Component

The problem statement is articulated, and the goals and objectives are set. The strategies component of the proposal systematically walks the prospective funder through the steps the organization proposes to carry out in order to accomplish its objectives. Strategies answer this key question: How will an organization actually accomplish the work for which it seeks funding?

Content of the Strategies Component

Strategies are detailed descriptions of the activities an organization will conduct to achieve the ends specified in its objectives. This section of the proposal should spell out the methods to be used and give the reasons for choosing them. Any research supporting the use of these methods – such as their previous successes or, if the methods are untested, data that support the assertion that these methods might prove successful – should be included. This section should also address whether the strategies selected are already in place within the organization and being replicated by the program, or whether they are new or being modified in some way, based on research or lessons learned. Finally, this section should describe the staff that will direct and implement the program and their qualifications, and identify the client population to be served, along with the reasons why this population was selected.

To develop the strategies component, answer the following questions:

1. What activities need to be carried out in order to meet the objectives?

2. What are the starting and ending dates of these activities?

3. Who has responsibility for completing each activity?

4. How will those served be identified? Or how will participants be selected? (The latter question is not applicable to all projects.)

5. How was this methodology determined to be the best one to solve the problem presented? Does it build on models already in existence, or is it a different approach? If it is different, why is it different? And why did the organization select it?

The strategies section should be realistic: the organization should be able to complete the proposed activities within the timeframe stated in the proposal, using the available resources. For proposals with multiple objectives and strategies, it is a good idea to include a timeline showing when each strategy will start and finish. The accompanying Sample Timeline for Alyson Eats shows one way to chart a nonprofit's activities on a timeline.

Tips for Writing the Strategies Component

- Align the organization's strategies to the program's objectives and problem statement.

- Tie the strategies to the resources being requested in the program budget. Each activity should match its corresponding cost exactly.

- Explain the rationale for choosing these strategies; talk in terms of research findings, best practices, expert opinion, community surveys or need assessments, and the organization's past experience with similar programs.

- Spell out the facilities and capital equipment that will be available for the project.

- Build various activity phases on top of one another to move the effort toward the desired results. Include a timeline if space allows.

- Be sure to discuss who will be served and how they will be identified.

- Do not assume that the funder knows about the nonprofit, its target audience, or what it proposes to accomplish.

WORKSHEET 5.1:
Sample Timeline (Abbreviated Version)

Activity and Lead Responsible	FY 19 Quarter 4	FY20 Quarter 1	FY20 Quarter 2	FY20 Quarter 3	FY20 Quarter 4
Confirm and coordinate food donations for FY 2020 (food resource team)	X	X	X		
Conduct volunteer outreach, recruitment and trainings in at least 12 community-based sites (volunteer manager)	X	X	X		
Confirm all FY20 food distribution sites and add at least three new ones in areas of greatest need identified through community survey (community outreach manager)	X	X			
Confirm food contributions and summer food distribution sites (food resource team)			X		
Plan Sharing Is Caring workshops including facilitators and confirm community-based training sites (community outreach manager)	X	X	X		
Hold Volunteer and Community Partner Recognition Day (volunteer manager)				X	X
Finalize Memorandum of Understanding (MOU) with Alyson High School for Food for Life Program (executive director)	X				
Work with Alyson High School to identify at least 30 students for program participation; ensure students have parental/guardian approval for participation (community outreach manager)		X	X		
Administer pretest to participants (Alyson High School staff)		X			
Hold year-end family meals and administer posttest (community outreach manager and Alyson High School staff)					X
Continuous evaluation of all Alyson Eats programs and FY 21 planning process.		X	X	X	X

Look over the sample Strategies Component for Alyson Eats. Then develop your organization's strategies by completing Worksheet 5.1, which should list the key elements of the organization's planned program. (See the Alyson Eats example worksheet 5.1B.) Finally, use the Strategies Review Questions to review the organization's methods in the same way the questions were deployed in the organization's program statement and goals and objectives.

Strategies

Alyson Eats provides most of our anti-hunger services through our three core programs, which we have tested and refined over the years and adapted to meet the changing needs of our communities.

EATING IS A RIGHT (EAR)

Alyson Eats created a large food pantry in a warehouse on the south side. Here we receive, inspect, organize and distribute boxes of healthful groceries for hungry families. The pantry is open for pick-up Wednesday through Sunday, from 6:00 a.m.–8:00 p.m. year-round to enable both day- and night-shift workers to stop in. Through the EAR program, we also distribute food boxes to central locations throughout the city, including schools, parks, churches/mosques/synagogues, and the main bus station. EAR is our oldest and most substantial program, requiring an extensive team of staff and volunteers in the warehouse, pantry, and behind the scenes, to source, inspect, transport, categorize, and distribute the food. As one tiny but vital example, we need a small army of volunteers – usually students – to fold and set up hundreds of cardboard boxes, which we buy in flat-packed bundles.

In 2020 we will distribute at least 9,000 boxes of nutritious food, each box weighing about 20 pounds and sufficient for 16 meals. This will total approximately 144,000 meals and 180,000 pounds of food during 2020. We do not ask for or keep track of our clients' names, but we estimate that the 9,000 food boxes will serve at least 3,000 households, since many of our clients are "repeat customers" who come in a few times a year for food supplies.

Goal: To provide access to 144,000 healthful meals for individuals and families in Alyson's south side.

Objective: The distribution of 180,000 pounds of nutritious food will reduce the risk of hunger for at least 3,000 households.

EVERY YOUNGSTER EATS (EYE)

During the summer months, Alyson Eats distributes ready-made lunches to childcare centers, nonprofit day camps, and so forth to make up for the free school lunches that children rely on during the school year. We partner with a local organization that helps parents organize childcare collectives, to make sure independent childcare providers have access to the EYE program's meals for the children they care for.

Goal: To reduce the summer school-lunch gap for 1,000 children.

Objective: 1,000 children will receive lunch five days a week from June through August (12 weeks), for a total of 60,000 meals.

SHARING IS CARING

This is our outreach program, through which we recruit and engage individuals, institutions, and businesses from across the city to participate in our anti-hunger activities. Our staff, volunteers, and board members seek to enroll businesses, grocery stores, caterers, and so forth to provide fresh, unopened goods to the EAR and EYE programs. We also help schools, congregations, Scout troops and others to organize food drives.

Sharing Is Caring is also the program through which we recruit and train a large portion of our volunteers. In many cases, these are people who work for the businesses and institutions that share their fresh food with us. We also recruit at schools, houses of worship, and through African American sororities, whose alumnae are among our strongest volunteer leaders. Every new volunteer goes through a three-hour training program and is assigned an experienced volunteer as a mentor. Each volunteer is asked to give at least 25 hours a month (e.g., one shift per week at the food pantry). We provide ongoing training, leadership development and education opportunities for volunteers so they can understand more deeply the causes of hunger and poverty and the power of informed citizens to change these dynamics. Although our staff members lead some of these programs, much of the training and teaching is done by local educators, by Alyson Eats' partner organizations in the advocacy and social change sectors, and by seasoned volunteers who have taken on important leadership roles. In 2020 we will recruit 40 additional volunteers, with the expectation that most volunteers will drop off or participate occasionally, but that we will be able to retain and develop 15 core volunteers from the group.

Goal: To increase volunteer engagement and participation by 30 percent.

Objective: Fifteen new core volunteers will contribute 4,500 hours of volunteer service.

FOOD FOR LIFE

This is a new program that we will test in 2020. The program is designed to help teenagers learn how to shop for and prepare simple, inexpensive, healthful meals from scratch, using widely available and/or seasonal ingredients. Of course, many young people in Alyson learn this from their own family members. Food for Life is for teenagers who don't have access to such experiences, such as the many south-side kids whose parents work two and three jobs.

During this first year, we will take three teams of 10 young people each on field trips to supermarkets and farmers markets, to familiarize them with the food products available in the wider world above 38th Street, and get them comfortable navigating the process of grocery shopping. We'll teach the young people skills such as how to read food labels, compare prices, and shop for sales, as well as basic cooking techniques. At the end of the year, students will invite their families to the Alyson Eats offices to enjoy a meal they themselves have shopped for and prepared.

But as we mentioned earlier in this proposal, "widely available" does not necessarily apply to Alyson residents who live in what is essentially a food desert, and seasonal produce may not be something they regularly encounter. A longer-term goal of Food for Life (beyond this one-year grant period) is to encourage local farmers markets both to establish more markets in the south side and to accept SNAP payments. Ultimately, we hope to introduce young people to an array of food choices that may be available to them in the near future, if not already, and to introduce food sellers to a whole new customer base they are not currently reaching.

Goal: To test the efficacy of a pilot program in improving eating habits and consumer awareness among high school students.

Objective: Thirty high school students enrolled in the pilot program will complete a pre- and post-assessment of the program's first year and discussion of how to refine the program in future years.

WORSHEET 5.1A:
Strategies Exercise

Activities – tasks and subtasks	Responsible – lead staff or team, volunteers	Resources Required	Start and Completion Dates

WORKSHEET 5.1B:
Strategies Exercise – Food for Life program

Activities – tasks and subtasks	Responsible – lead staff or team, volunteers	Resources Required	Start and Completion Dates
Finalize MOU with Alyson High School (AHS)	Exec. Director	Draft MOU, one-page summary of program	9/1/19 9/30/19
Identify 30 students to participate	Community outreach manager (with AHS staff)	List of qualifications for participants Permission form for parents/guardians	1/10/20 1/31/20
Administer pre-test to participants	Community outreach manager (with AHS staff)	Online survey Reserve computer time in school library	2/10/20 3/2/20

Strategies Review Questions

1. Do the strategies discussed in the proposal derive logically from the problem statement and the goals and objectives?

2. Do the strategies present the program activities to be undertaken?

3. Has the grantseeker explained why they selected the specific strategies or activities?

4. Has the grantseeker explained the timing and order of the specific activities?

5. Is it clear who will perform specific activities? And do their credentials and/or experience demonstrate that they are appropriate to carry out the activities of the program?

6. Given the organization's projected resources, are the proposed activities feasible?

If an organization is following along with each step, including testing each proposal component against the questions at the end of each, it is now in a prime position to be successful in the next step: developing the evaluation component, which is Step 6.

Step 6
Preparing the Evaluation Component

EVERYTHING COMPLETED UP TO THIS POINT in the development of the organization's proposal (problem statement, goals, objectives, and strategies) naturally leads to this component. The evaluation answers critical questions for both the organization and the funder, such as:

- Was the program successful?

- Did it do what it was designed to do?

- What did the organization learn from this experience that can be leveraged?

- What didn't work – and why?

- What's different in the community or the lives of those targeted as a result of the program?

Before writing this section of a grant proposal, it is essential for an organization to plan how it will evaluate what it proposes to do. This step explores learning how to write an effective evaluation plan so that the organization can demonstrate the success of its program and measure program impact – and capture the lessons learned. An exercise will help grantseekers think about what their evaluation plans should contain.

Definitions

Impact: The change an organization creates as a result of its program activities.

Leverage: A method of grantmaking practiced by some foundations, when they give a small amount of money with the express purpose of attracting funding from other sources or providing the organization with the tools it needs to raise other kinds of funds. Sometimes known as the "multiplier effect."[1] (An organization may also use leverage, for instance by enabling other organizations to replicate successful approaches it has developed, thus using one effort to build strength for other efforts.)

Purpose of the Evaluation Component

Evaluation is a process that determines the impact, effectiveness, and efficiency of a program. It reveals what worked and – equally important – what did not. Funders expect to hear from organizations how they define and measure the success of a program, whether the funder explicitly requests an evaluation or not. Yet the primary purpose of an evaluation should not be to satisfy a funder, but to help an organization assess the effectiveness of its work and plan for the program's future. For that reason, how a program will be evaluated must be determined prior to its implementation, so that the organization can build evaluation measurements into the program plan. The organization then will be well-positioned to produce, at the end of a grant period, an organized and objective assessment documenting the return on investment for funders and the realized benefits to the community the organization serves.

Definition

Return on investment (ROI): The amount of benefit (return) based on the amount of resources (funds, hours of work) used to produce it.

The Virtues of Evaluation

First, a good evaluation component strengthens the proposal from the funder's perspective. Grantseekers are asking potential grantmakers to invest in their organizations and programs – and they are asking the funders' staffs to be their advocates. They want the funders to bet on the fact that the world will be improved in some specific way as a result of the nonprofits' proposed programs. Essentially, the programs serve to test a hypothesis: "If we do this, then that will happen." A solid evaluation component in a proposal reassures funders that the organizations are interested, as the funders are, in learning whether this hypothesis is correct.

Second, through evaluation, organizations will learn about the programs' strengths and areas of weakness. The process of thinking through the evaluation design can strengthen a program before it is even implemented. From there, organizations can take the knowledge gained through an actual evaluation and share it with staff and volunteers to improve programs as they are being implemented. This knowledge may also be shared with others in the field so that they, too, can learn from the lessons of the program's work.

The third benefit is to the public – the impact. Dollars granted from foundations and corporate-giving programs are dollars dedicated to charitable good; therefore, with each grant an organization receives, it becomes a recipient of public trust. Because of that, the organization has an obligation to ensure that its programs are actually having a positive impact on the community or on the organization's target audience. Evaluation is one of the strongest and most effective tools any nonprofit has to verify and document that it is indeed fulfilling its obligation to make a positive impact on the community it serves.

Definition

Hypothesis: The assumed proposition that is tested in a research process.

Internal or External Evaluation

Some foundations will allow organizations to designate a certain amount of money or a certain percentage (generally from 5 to 10 percent, sometimes more) of the total program budget for evaluation; others will not. Therefore, organizations need to consider how they will evaluate their programs for the purpose of documenting results, findings, and lessons learned. There are some organizations that will spend time up front designing their evaluation components with the confidence that they have both the staffing and the expertise in place to objectively handle the evaluation internally. Other organizations will decide to engage an outside evaluator; among the most common reasons for doing so are that the organization (1) lacks expertise among the staff, (2) has the staff expertise but lacks the staff time to dedicate to evaluation, or (3) wants the evaluation to be deemed as objective as possible. Keep in mind that even if an organization hires an outside evaluator, it needs to reserve some staff time for the evaluation. An outside expert cannot conduct an evaluation without significant participation from the organization.

Organizations should provide some background information in the proposal that indicates whether they plan to evaluate the program internally or hire an external evaluator. The proposal budget should also reflect an expense line item for evaluation.

Content of the Evaluation Component

To design an evaluation, one first needs to consider the organization's definition of success – the "so what?" factor. Then one must have a clear understanding of how the activities described in the proposal will lead to the expected outcomes. Finally, one needs to identify the aspects of the program for which it is most important that the organization can assess how well they worked – and why they did or didn't work.

Organizations conduct evaluations primarily to accomplish five goals:

1. Find out whether the hypothesis was correct: Did what the organization proposed actually do what the organization expected it would?

2. Determine whether the strategies that were specified were indeed used and the objectives met.

3. Determine whether the organization's work made an impact on the problem identified.

4. Obtain feedback from the clients served and other members of the community.

5. Make midcourse corrections along the way to increase the program's chances of success.

When preparing the evaluation section of the proposal, answering the following questions will help frame the description:

1. What is the purpose of the organization's evaluation?

2. How will the findings be used?

3. What will the organization know after the evaluation that it does not know now?

4. What will the organization do after the evaluation that it cannot do now because of lack of information?

5. How will the lives of the people or community served by the organization be better?

6. Did the organization use the funder's investment wisely? Were the funds effectively managed or leveraged?

7. Was the program budget accurate, or did the program components end up costing significantly more or less that the organization expected?

This workbook provides a broad overview that can help grantseekers determine the parameters most appropriate for the program. Generally, there are two approaches to data collection: quantitative methods and qualitative methods.

Quantitative methods are methods to quantify (measure or count) data. Using this method, an organization collects data that can be analyzed statistically, via averages, means, percentiles, and the like. It can help an organization quantify *how much* it did – how many people did it train? How many meals did it deliver? These analyses allow organizations to make statements about cause-and-effect relationships. Employ quantitative methods in order to:

• Understand the quantities or frequency of particular aspects of a program (such as number of enrollees or number of dropouts).

- Determine whether an organization's actions directly caused a particular result.

- Compare two different methods seeking to achieve the same outcomes.

- Establish numerical baselines that can be used in before-and-after comparisons (through such means as pretests and posttests, and quarterly or yearly follow-ups).

Qualitative methods, in contrast, are based on direct contact with the people involved with a program. These methods consist of interviews (group or individual), observation (direct or field), and personal stories told both in writing and in photos or videos, as well as review of selected documents. This approach can help organizations examine *what it did* and *why it mattered*. Employ qualitative methods in order to:

- Understand feelings or opinions about a program among participants, staff, or community members.

- Gain insight into how patterns of relationships in the program unfold.

- Gather multiple perspectives to understand the whole picture.

- Identify approximate indicators that clients are moving in the "right" direction.

In other words, pretests and posttests are not the only measures of success. By taking the time upfront to think strategically, an organization can come up with an evaluation design that incorporates both quantitative and qualitative methods.

A good evaluation lets both the funder and the nonprofit know whether the organization's activities are achieving their desired effect. An evaluation that is "just for show" or designed merely to please a funder – and not to answer real questions that organizations should be asking themselves about their work's effectiveness – are a waste of time and resources.

Take a look at the evaluation component prepared for the Alyson Eats organization, which uses both quantitative and qualitative data to assess its long-running programs. The organization is also testing a new program, and will seek outside help to design an evaluation for it.

Sample Evaluation Component

[Quantitative data] Our three core programs have specific annual goals, objectives, and outcomes to achieve during 2020:

- The EAR program seeks to provide 144,000 nutritious meals totaling 180,000 pounds of food for individuals and families in Alyson's south side.

- The EYE program aims to provide lunch five days a week to 1,000 children over the summer, for a total of 60,000 meals; and

- The Sharing Is Caring program strives to recruit 15 new volunteers in order to increase volunteer engagement by 30 percent.

Because we have been conducting these programs for over a decade, we've established a rigorous system of quarterly check-ins to track our progress toward the annual goals.

[Qualitative data] In addition to these quantifiable benchmarks, Alyson Eats regularly seeks input from our partners, volunteers, and the people we serve. These inputs range from quarterly conversations in which volunteers and staff are invited to talk about what they think is working well and what could be improved, to a series of poster boards we display on the walls of our food pantry that enable our clients to tell us, through the use of colored stick-on dots, how they think we're doing and what we could do better. Thanks to our historical and current partnership with the university, particularly the School of Social Work, students frequently work with Alyson Eats to create evaluation instruments and conduct assessments of our programs as part of their field practice. We take all of these evaluations seriously, and continually refine our programs to meet the needs and standards the assessments reveal.

Public Funding: Evaluation

Evaluation requirements for public funding applications vary widely depending on the funding source, type of program being funded, and other factors. For example, many federal – and some state and local – proposals require applicants to include plans to engage outside evaluators to conduct rigorous programmatic assessments, and applicants can and should include these evaluation costs in their proposed budget, as allowable in the Request for Applications and other regulations.

Even in cases in which an outside evaluator is not required, if resources allow, your public funding evaluation section should be developed and/or reviewed by someone with expertise in program evaluation. This could be a staff person, a board member, consultant, or other organizational partner who has this expertise, or even an instructor or graduate level student at a local community college or other institution of higher education.

If you are developing the evaluation section yourself, be sure that the evaluation ties directly to the goals and objectives and is represented in the logic model, workplan, and/or timeline. Some public funders may also ask about your plans to publish or disseminate the findings of your evaluation – be sure to include a detailed plan for this aspect of the evaluation in the logic model, workplan and/or timeline as well.

Answer the questions in Worksheet 6.1 to begin planning the evaluation section. Then review the section with the Evaluation Review Questions.

WORKSHEET 6.1A:
Evaluation Planning Questionnaire

1. What questions will the organization's evaluation activities seek to answer?

2. What are the evaluation plans and time frames?

    (a) What kinds of data will be collected?

    (b) At what points?

    (c) Using what strategies or instruments?

    (d) Using what comparison group or baseline, if any?

3. If the intention is to study a sample of participants, how will this sample be selected?

WORKSHEET 6.1A:
Evaluation Planning Questionnaire (Continued)

4. What procedures will be used to determine whether the program was implemented as planned?

5. Who will conduct the evaluation?

6. Who will receive the results?

7. How does this program or project define success?

Evaluation Review Questions

1. Does the evaluation section focus on assessing the project results?

2. Does it explain how the evaluation will assess the efficiency of program methods?

3. Does it describe who will be evaluated and what will be measured?

4. Does it specify what information will be collected in the evaluation process?

5. Does it state who will be responsible for making the assessments?

6. Does it discuss how the information and conclusions will be used to improve the program?

7. Does it provide the organization's definition of success?

If the program is successful and the organization is able to document that success through evaluation, the organization will probably want to continue implementing the program. Step 7 addresses the need to plan now for program sustainability beyond the initial funding.

Note

1. Definition courtesy of Council on Foundations, "Glossary of Philanthropic Terms," https://www.cof.org/content/glossary-philanthropic-terms.

Step 7
Developing a Statement of Sustainability

PART OF THE CASE THAT GRANTSEEKERS must make to potential funders is that they have a plan to fully fund their organization and/or program now and in the future. Funders want to know what strategies organizations have developed to build a sustainable pool of grant funding, including other funders who have been secured or identified, individual donors who support the program, and other resources that are being leveraged including in-kind support and partnerships. In this step, grantseekers learn how to develop the sustainability statement and identify, through exercises and examples, potential sources of ongoing support that are best for the program.

Content of the Sustainability Statement

The sustainability statement should reflect whether the proposal is seeking general operating, program, capital or equipment, or capacity-building funding. (Reminder: these types of requests were defined in the Overview Section). Whatever the type of request, the grantseeker should lay out the plan to sustain the organization, program, or capital expenditure in the long term. In the case of a capacity-building grant, the grantseeker should explain how the additional capacity can be implemented or sustained.

Funders pay much more attention to this section than most grantseekers would probably suspect, because they will have a vested interest in the organization's or project's success *beyond their funding*. Therefore, this section of the proposal should provide a framework that shows how the nonprofit plans to raise money and leverage resources beyond the funder's investment, as well as who on the organization's staff will be responsible for making this plan happen.

For *general operating grants* – the sustainability statement should address: the organization's history in meeting revenue needs, future plans for diversifying funding from a variety of sources, the experience of its staff – including any staff specifically dedicated to development – and board in fundraising efforts, and any in-kind or donated resources that count toward its revenue goal (such as donated food and volunteer time in the case of Alyson Eats).

For *project- or program-specific grants* – the sustainability statement should address: the history of the funding for the program, or in the case of a new program a rationale for why and how the resources will be raised and by whom. The sustainability statement can also include the organization's success in other fundraising efforts by including the information listed under general operating grants.

For *capital or equipment (major equipment purchases or building renovations and expansion) grants* – the sustainability statement should help funders understand the associated costs for operating the new equipment, for maintaining the new building, or for increasing services if building expansion results in program expansion. Funders will want to be sure that the organization can sustain the capital or equipment expenditure that their investment will support. So, for example, if a funder supports the expansion of technology through the purchase of hardware, your sustainability plan should address how that hardware will be maintained and that you have a plan to support the needed software and infrastructure (such as high-speed Internet) to make the hardware usable.

For *capacity-building grants* – the sustainability statement should help funders understand how the organization will support the capacity it has grown. For example, a request might be made for a capacity-building grant to increase the organization's fundraising ability by hiring a consultant to create a development plan. Once the plan is created – and the grant is expended – how does the organization plan to pay for the actual implementation of the new development plan? Does the organization have the staff and other resources to implement the plan?

In building the case for sustainability, here are some of the sources grantseekers can discuss in their strategy:

- *Grants from other foundations and corporations.* A nonprofit can seek continuing support from those foundations and corporations that fund ongoing programs. If your organization or program is effective and you properly cultivate and steward relationships with funders, they will often continue to support organizations beyond their initial investment. Once again, both the funder research along with the relationship building, as outlined in Step 2, have a direct impact on the outcome of continued funding.

- *Support from individual donors.* Developing support from individual donors is a key strategy for nonprofits, although it takes a particular set of skills and organizational assets to do effectively. Check the Resource section on places to learn more about developing individual donors, including online through crowd-funding and other strategies.

- *Fees for service.* Some organizations generate revenue in other ways, such as providing consulting services in its areas of expertise or, for example, receiving a fee from a school to provide afterschool tutoring programs. If a nonprofit opts to ask clients to pay fees, the fee scale should be explained and shown in the proposal.

- *Sales of items or activities.* A nonprofit might be able to set up an income-producing situation, such as a gift shop or thrift store. In addition, it might be able to sell publications, concert recordings, or educational activities. Revenues generated from these sales might cover some costs of the program. If this route is taken, a clear expense and revenue projection should be a part of the proposal. (*Please note*: Organizations need to check with both legal counsel and accounting counsel to ensure that any revenue-generating ventures launched are set up and monitored in accordance with IRS guidelines.)

A typical mistake that grantseekers make in their proposals is writing a vague sustainability statement, something to the effect of "future funding will come from a mix of sources such as other grants and individual support." Be sure to take time to develop and write a compelling plan for long-term support that will help funders feel secure in your ability to be around for the long haul.

Tips for Writing the Sustainability Component

Helpful Hint

Sell it! If an organization has examples of other instances in which it successfully continued programs beyond initial funding, this would be the place to share such information, because it speaks to the organization's credibility not only in launching programs but also in maintaining them.

Many funders ask for this component in their grant guidelines; others do not. Whether or not this component is required, grantseekers should include some information on sources of support for the project's future. The more specific grantseekers are in this section, the more confidence they will inspire in potential funders that the project will continue beyond their grant, thereby maximizing the impact of their investment.

Take a look at the Sample Sustainability Component to see what the Alyson Eats has planned for the sustainability of its program.

Sample Sustainability Component for Alyson Eats

Nothing would please Alyson Eats more than to go out of business because there's no longer a need for our services. Short of that, we have a robust fundraising operation.

Our budget for 2020 is $1.3 million. We have commitments totaling 85 percent of this amount. Of our current commitments, approximately 57 percent are in-kind donations of volunteer work, food and facilities; 42 percent are donations from individuals, including our volunteers and their friends, and from institutions and foundations. With few exceptions, these are local and regional funders like the Future Foundation. We take it as a vote of confidence that the people who see our work close-up are the ones most moved to invest in our ongoing efforts. In the past few years, a new population of individual donors has emerged: people who once relied on our services, and now are on firm enough footing economically that they can turn around and donate to our programs. Although we value and appreciate every donation, the gifts from former clients mean the most to us.

Alyson Eats has yet to raise $197,016, which represents about 15 percent of our 2020 budget. A grant at the requested level from the Future Foundation would reduce our revenue gap by approximately 25 percent.

Public Funding

Public funding applications may or may not have a dedicated section that addresses sustainability. Public funders often want to understand how the program will be supported once the grant ends. They also want to understand that public funds are being leveraged to raise dollars from the private sector. If there is a sustainability question(s), the tips provided in this section will be equally helpful for public funding applications. As in the case of foundations, you want to be as specific as possible. And, as always, follow the specific guidelines outlined in the request for application.

Answering the Sustainability Review Questions will assist in developing the component of the proposal that deals with future funding.

Sustainability Review Questions

1. Is it the organization's intent to have the program continue after the initial grant funding is gone?

2. If yes, does the sustainability component of the proposal present a plan for securing future funding for the program?

3. Does it discuss future funding strategies or earned-income strategies?

4. If the organization is requesting a multiyear grant, did it show that the organization will have a decreasing reliance on grant support each year? (Grantmakers are more inclined to make a multiyear grant to nonprofits that assume greater financial responsibility for the project each year, rather than asking the funder to maintain the same level of funding each year.)

The grantseeker has now developed a thoughtful statement of sustainability. It is time to develop a financial document to accompany the grant proposal—the grant budget, which is discussed in Step 8.

Step 8
Developing the Proposal Budget

THIS STEP PROVIDES THE BASIC TOOLS to develop an effective program (or proposal) budget. It is important to approach this step in a way that tells a story. Yes, a budget is the proposal narrative reflected in numbers. Approaching the development of a budget through this lens will ensure continuity. This chapter will also introduce terms and definitions that will help grantseekers to understand the various elements of a budget. Finally, this step provides budget development information for both foundations and public funding grant opportunities.

General Budget Overview

When applying for grants from foundations, typically one of two types of budgets will be requested, consistent with the type of grant funding being sought: a *general support* (GS), which is also referred to as *general operating support* (GOS), budget or a *program* (or *project*) budget.

General Support Budget

A general support budget details the income and expenses for the fiscal year – or the grant period – in which the funding is being requested. It should directly reflect the overall goals, values, and intended impact of the organization.

A few basic guidelines include:

Organize income and expenses into line items that match the work and activities. This is where reflecting the overall goals, values, and intended impact of the organization is important, and reinforces the organization's commitment to the work.

Capture all staff costs. If there is staff, create a line item for employee benefits and taxes, including payroll tax. Social Security, Medicare, and unemployment insurance are all necessary overhead expenses. Other common employee expenses are medical insurance, and disability insurance. These expenses are typically pooled for all employees into a single line item.

Include D and O liability insurance. Many grant funders require that an organization have directors and officers liability insurance. This insurance covers board members who suffer injuries or property damage, or who might be involved in a lawsuit for sexual harassment, discrimination, mismanagement of funds, or wrongful termination. It is important to reflect this expense as a line item in the budget.

Little things add up, so be sure to include them. Annual operating budgets should include *indirect costs* such as accounting, auditing, property and liability insurance, evaluation, and portions of staff time required to administer projects, as allowable by the funder. Grant-funded activities can easily eat into general overhead budget.

Create a modest cushion. Unexpected expenses are an everyday part of nonprofit organizations. Include a bit of cushion in an annual operating budget for such expenses and shortfalls. A cushion is particularly important for start-up organizations that may lack predictable income streams. A few funders will allow a "miscellaneous" line item for this purpose. In general, though, you can include a small cushion to existing line items (although not line items like personnel that are based on specific salaries for a specific number of staff).

Helpful Hint

Be sure to research what an acceptable indirect cost rate should be. Some funders have already established their allowable indirect cost rate for any grants they fund. For instance, if a funder will only allow an indirect cost rate of 12 percent, but the organization's indirect cost rate is 20 percent, the program will have to offset the 8 percent loss in overhead costs in other areas of the budget.

Program Budget

An organization may have several programs that it is responsible to manage throughout a given year. A program budget is a subset of the annual operating budget and will therefore fall under the purview of an organization's annual operating budget. A programmatic budget is specific to a body of work and should only reflect the costs associated with said body of work. Even a single-issue organization may have several different programs it has implemented in service to achieving its mission. There may be programs specific to different geographies, demographics, and other factors that would warrant separate program budgets. If this were the case, each program would have its own separate budget reflecting the expenses associated with each one.

For the purpose of this workbook and the sample proposal used throughout, the focus will be on a GS budget that will accompany the proposal.

Basics of a GS Budget

Development of a general support budget should involve the executive director, as well as the finance staff person. The budget includes all expenses of the organization and is essentially the organization's annual operating budget.

The following is a list of stages that are necessary to develop a program budget.

Stage 1: Review, Research, and Organize

Stage 2: Develop the Budget

Stage 3: Review, Update, and Review Again

Stage 4: Develop the Budget Narrative

Incorporating these stages into a budget-development process will ensure a comprehensive general support budget that reflects thoughtfulness and planning. Funders will pay close attention to a grantseeker's efforts to adhere to their budget requirements, document projected revenues, and research relevant expenses for their proposed grant request.

Stage 1: Review, Research, and Organize

The first stage is a two-part process that starts the budget formulation process. Part one involves reading the grant application for understanding and clarity, and part two explains how to research and organize the information to be included in the budget. Let's begin by understanding the grant application budget review process.

Review the Grant Application for Budget Requirements

Before investing in the development of the budget and selecting a budget tool (example: MS Excel or Google Spreadsheet), it is important to read through the grant application and determine what is required. It is standard for funders to provide or specify a document or tool that should be used to capture the budget, as well as to identify or list the information to be included as attachments. As a potential grantee, it is important to follow the instructions provided in the grant application, supplementing it with any information (as allowed by the funder) that will make the organization's financial needs clear.

Important items to consider in the grant application guidelines before developing the budget may include the following:

- A budget template with instructions including whether it is mandatory to use the form.

- Instructions on the budget categories or level of the budget details and how those details should be recorded.

- Items that should not be included in the budget.

- If a *budget narrative* should be included and in what format (see the definition later in this chapter).

- Clarity around the percentage of "indirect" or "overhead" an organization can include in the budget. This will vary greatly from funder to funder, as well as for public funding at the local, state, and federal levels. See the public funding section of this chapter for more details.

Although this stage might appear tedious, it is necessary so that grantseekers develop budgets that mirror the narrative in the written proposals. This alignment between written proposal and corresponding budget will more fully sustain a funder's attention, and shows that the organization has its financial house in order. By following directions, an organization demonstrates its level of commitment to effectively stewarding the funding being requested.

Now that the budget instructions and specific requirements have been properly read and digested, it is time to begin to research and organize budget details.

Helpful Hint

Consider using a spreadsheet to document the information researched and help track and organize the information collected.

Research and Organize Budget Information

The process of researching, collecting, and organizing the budget data is often underestimated when developing the budget. Before beginning to develop the budget, there are several actions that should occur:

- Identify the types of revenues and expenses that are included in the organization's budget.

- Research, develop, and collect estimates for revenues and expenses.
- Organize the data to facilitate the budget-development process (next step).
- Keep in mind that budgets consist of good faith estimates – a best guess based on solid research.

Remember: If an organization wants its budget to tell a compelling numerical story of their grant proposal, it needs to be both thorough and accurate. This will take time, so build that into the grant development timeline.

Stage 2: Develop the Budget

Now that the budget requirements for the grant proposal are clear and budget information is organized, it is time to develop the budget. The next step is to deploy the information gathered from Stage 1. It is safe to assume that the funders will provide an online proposal budget spreadsheet, so the more organizations are familiar with spreadsheet software, the easier it will be to navigate the online (and paper for any outliers) budget spreadsheets.

Establish the Budget Period

Every budget has a beginning and ending period called the *budget period*. This budget period for a grant will be one of these three:

1. The organization's fiscal year
2. The program year (specific to program grants)
3. The grant period (which funders sometimes define)

For the purpose of the example in this work, the budget period for the Alyson Eats Future Foundation proposal is January 1, 2020 through December 31, 2020.

Helpful Hint

Keep in mind that some grants may cover multiple years, and require a multiyear budget. Make sure the budget is consistent from year to year and includes adjustments, like cost-of-living adjustments for staff and possible product increases.

Estimate Revenues and Expenses

In Stage 1, all revenues and expenses that should be included in the budget were identified. At this point, most revenues and expenses will be estimates and should be documented as such. There are instances when actual revenue and expense amounts are known and, if so, those should be included as actuals.

Revenue is income identified and/or already committed for the program such as memberships, fee-for-service, other grants, and other fundraising endeavors such as special events and individual giving. Depending on the grant, an organizational budget may contain several different revenue streams. A list of potential revenue sources includes other foundation support, government funding, and individual funds. In addition, items like in-kind donations of supplies, services, and human capital and other volunteer services should also be listed as revenue sources.

The revenue sources included in the budget should be estimated according to the expected or known revenue stream. For instance, if the revenue is based on memberships or fee-for-service, the amount can be calculated as follows:

$$\text{Revenue} = \text{quantity of the memberships/fee-for-service} \times \text{price of membership/fee-for-service}$$

or

$$\text{Revenue} = \text{Amount assessed for membership fees and/or services rendered} \times \text{expected number of members}$$

Example: Revenue Budget Table for Alyson Eats	
Revenues	**Projected**
GS support from foundations (Open Communities Fund; Southside Community Foundation; Jane Irving Family Foundation; individual donors)	$250,000
Restricted/Programmatic support	$225,000
Abundant Living Community Church	$10,000
Membership and T-shirt sales	$10,000
Facilities costs in-kind	$10,000
Volunteers – 50 × $500 mo. each average (in-kind support)	$300,000
In-kind food donations	$350,000
Total	**$1,155,000**

Expenses are the costs of those items required to sustain the program. They are a critical piece of the budget because they identify the costs necessary to manage and sustain a program. Expenses can be recorded in two categories – direct and indirect costs.

Direct Costs

Direct costs include all expenses that can be identified and charged, such as personnel, fringe benefits, consultants, subcontractors, travel, equipment, supplies and materials, communications, computer time, and publication charges.

These costs should be itemized in the budget, with the exception of the staffing line item, which should include staff and fringe. In Stage 1, we discussed researching, developing, and collecting revenue and expense estimates. This section further highlights why this stage is necessary.

Because these costs are directly related to the operations of the organization, they should be easy to identify. Here is a short list of potential expenses that may be listed as direct costs or expenses:

- Staff and fringe

- Travel and lodging

- Supplies and materials

- Equipment and technology

- Food and beverages

- Facility rental

Calculating direct costs should be kept simple and straightforward. For instance, Alyson Eats employs nine people: one management staff, three full-time staff, and five part-time staff:

Example: Estimated Salary Table for Alyson Eats

Role	No. of Staff	Monthly Wages	Yearly Total*
Executive Director	1	$5,000	$60,000
Lead Program Staff	3	$3,500 ea./$10,500	$126,000
Half-time staff	5	$2,000 ea./$10,000	$120,000
Fringe for staff*	9		$85,680
Volunteers – in-kind**	50	$500 ea./$25,000	$300,000
Total	59 (50 vols)	$50,500	$691,680

*Fringe benefits are calculated on the nine paid staff only at 28 percent of $306,000, which comes to $85,680. The $306,000 amount is the sum of the Executive Director, three Lead Program Staff, and five Half-Time Staff salaries.
**Volunteer line represents an in-kind contribution. Since volunteers are not staff, no fringe expenses are associated with this line item.
Yearly total calculation = Monthly Wages × 12 Months + Fringe line item

The "Total" amount listed in the table (minus the $300,000 for volunteers) is the number that will be included in the Salary row of the budget spreadsheet.

Example: Alyson Eats Annual Operating Expenses FY2020

Expenses	Projected
Staffing and Fringe (28%) for nine permanent staff (one manager, three full time program, five half-time)	$391,680
Facilities – in-kind	$10,000
Board support and D&O Insurance	$10,000
Volunteer support (in-kind)	$300,000
Food and Supplies	$150,000
Food and Supplies (in-kind)	$350,000
Programmatic supplies and marketing materials	$20,000
Evaluation	$5,000
Indirect expenses*	$115,336
Expense Subtotal	**$1,352,016**

*Indirect expense amount is calculated at 20 percent of all non-in-kind line items.

Helpful Hint

In some instances, personnel costs are split between programs because staff may spend only a portion of their time on a project. If this is the case, the personnel costs should be determined by using the percentage of time spent on the program budget in question.

Indirect Costs

Many established nonprofits already have an indirect rate that can be applied to the budget. This is a helpful way to be sure indirect costs are being appropriately allocated across programmatic areas within the organization.

Indirect costs – also known as overhead costs – are costs that are incurred for common or joint objectives of the organization (or program), and which, therefore, are shared throughout every programmatic and operational budget. This includes, but is not limited to, building operations and maintenance, laboratory space, library service, utilities, and administrative services. The following is a short list of potential indirect costs or expenses. Indirect costs may include the following:

- Utilities
- Information technology support
- Audit or legal staff
- Rent
- Administrative support
- Equipment rental

This estimate is usually determined by using an indirect cost rate.

Helpful Hint

Let's assume the organization's indirect cost rate equals 20 percent. Because this rate was already established within the organization, Alyson Eats' indirect costs can be calculated. If Alyson Eats' direct costs total $576,680, for example, the indirect cost amount that will be included in the budget is $576,680 × 20 percent or $115,336.

Keep in mind that the indirect cost rate calculation is only useful when there are some expenses that are shared among programs or projects and the organization is trying to determine only those programs' indirect costs.

In-Kind Support/Donated Goods and Services

Many organizations operate programs using a combination of paid employees and purchased goods and services, combined with volunteers and donated goods and services. The volunteer time and donated goods and services are considered support and are a vital part of the budget process. They should be included as both revenues *and* expenses where applicable. The following (short) list of items can be considered when including in-kind contributions:

- Volunteer or staff time of those unaffiliated with the organization and therefore not included in the staff budget line. Note that some companies participate in what are referred to as "loaned executive" programs, where company staff wanting to contribute their time and expertise to directly benefit the community are "loaned" to a qualified nonprofit organization that can effectively absorb the additional support.

- General volunteers.

- Donated services, including food, printing, marketing, accounting, and other services.

- Donated items including office equipment, vehicles, and other tangible items used for the program.

- Donation of office or facility space (rent, utilities, and renovations).

There are several factors that should be considered when estimating the costs of these items. For instance, volunteer and staff time estimates can be calculated using the average amount an organization would pay someone providing the same or like service multiplied by the number of hours performing the service, as shown in the formula below:

Volunteer/staff time estimate = $ of service if purchased

(in the marketplace) × number of hours volunteered

In-kind contributions should not be ignored or taken lightly during the budget process. There are many benefits to including these items in your budget, including:

- Reduces the overall cash outlay for program expenses.

- Expands resource capacity to sustain an organization's program.

- Opens the door for community partners to learn about and support the organization's program or cause.

- Demonstrates to the funder the value of the donor and volunteer contributions.

As mentioned earlier, in-kind contributions are typically shown as revenues and expenses to create a net-zero effect. For example, if a volunteer contributes $2,000 worth of her time, that amount should be shown as $2,000 in volunteer support revenue *and* $2,000 in volunteer support expenses.

It is important that in-kind contributions are net-zero when balancing the budget because noncash income should not be used to offset cash expenses.

Record Budget Information   Once the budget categories have been identified and researched and revenues and expenses finalized, it is time to record this information. The information should be listed in an easy to follow format, preferably using a spreadsheet tool selected early in the process.

Be sure to follow the grant application guidelines regarding the format in which this information should be recorded. Not following instructions is the surest way for a proposal to be declined.

Stage 3: Review, Update, and Review Budget Again

This stage in the budget-development process is a commonsense yet often-missed step. Simply put, grantseekers need to review the budget for formula and number errors. This is a necessary step that should not be neglected. Build in the time for the finance staff person to:

1. Double-check that the staffing and fringe are accurately allocated to the program.

2. Ensure that all other line items are appropriate.

3. Avoid missing expenses that should otherwise be included in a GS grant budget.

4. Make sure organizational overhead is included at the maximum level allowed.

5. Ensure that the format of the budget is clear, understandable, and that it fits correctly within the grant guidelines.

6. And double-check that all calculations are correct.

Stage 4: Develop the Budget Narrative

Now that the budget spreadsheet is complete and the numbers reviewed and verified, a budget narrative (sometimes called *budget justification*) should be developed to explain how the numbers were derived, as well as verify what the numbers represent.

After the budget is developed, a detailed narrative of the significant items in the budget should be written. In its simplest form, this document provides a written narrative for budget items that are not self-explanatory, and require some context about how expenses and revenues were derived and why they are needed. For instance, a line item that says "Consultants—$10,000" tells the funder little, but a narrative saying "two consultants at $5,000 each to videotape the classroom sessions" makes it clear. A budget narrative shows that the organization put thought and care into the revenues and expenses included in the budget. Here is a simple example of what Alyson Eats' budget justification may look like:

Sample Budget Justification

The total budget required to support Alyson Eats for the 2020 fiscal year is $1,352,016, inclusive of $660,000 in in-kind volunteer support, food, and supplies. Additional details of the budget are described below:

Alyson Eats has outlined its sources of projected revenue needed to reduce hunger among the people we serve for one year. The following is a list of committed funding for the year to date:

Example: Revenue Budget Table for Alyson Eats

Revenues	Projected
GOS support from foundations (Open Communities Fund; Southside Community Foundation; Jane Irving Family Foundation; individual donors)	$250,000
Restricted/Programmatic support	$225,000
Abundant Living Community Church	$10,000
Membership and T-shirt sales	$10,000
Facilities costs (in-kind)	$10,000
Volunteers – 50 × $500 mo. each average (in-kind support)[*]	$300,000
In-kind food donations	$350,000
Total	**$1,155,000**

[*] Alyson Eats receives generous volunteer support from 50 dedicated individuals, which is valued at $500 per month per volunteer, for a total of $300,000 in in-kind staffing.

Again, the budget justification is typically documented in a narrative format. Depending on the funder's requirements, the budget narrative could be included as a paragraph in the proposal, added to the bottom of the budget document, or presented as a supplement to the budget. Because there is likely to be limited space, explanations should be concise and explain those items in the budget that require further clarification.

The Budget: Final Thoughts

Now that the building blocks for developing the proposal budget are in place, there are a few additional points that should be remembered:

- Read and understand the type of budget the funder is requiring for the grant application.

- Provide a true and honest picture of expected revenues and expenses.

- Justify in writing, to the extent possible, any budget items that stand out as unusual or costly.

Remember: focus on telling a story with the budget that directly reflects the written proposal. The presentation of the budget is equally as important as the presentation of the overall program that will be supported by the grant.

Program Budget Do's and Don'ts

The following is a list of Do's and Don'ts when developing the grant application's program budget.

Do . . .
- Understand that a budget is an important part of the grant application process.

- Read the grant application for budget requirements, including formats and specific instructions.

- Identify elements to include in the budget based on organizational needs.

- Collect and record data to substantiate revenues and expenses listed in the budget.

- If allowed, provide a budget narrative to explain any major funding variances or requests.

- Itemize revenues and expenses to the extent the funder's budget template allows.

Don't . . .

- Overlook the importance of developing a logical and reasonable budget based on the funder's instructions.

- Include items that are not specifically requested in the grant application.

- Lump all revenues and expenses together; rather, itemize for clarity.

- Forget to review and check all amounts, formulas, and calculations in the final document before submitting.

Take some time to fill out Worksheet 8.1 to help organize the information that will go into your budget. Once you've drafted a budget, ask yourself the Budget Review Questions.

WORKSHEET 8.1:
Revenue and Expense Budget

On the Web

	Cash Required	In-Kind Contributions	Total Budget
REVENUE			
Foundations			
Government			
Corporations			
Individual contributions			
Donated printing and supplies			
Volunteer services			
Other (specify):			
Total revenue			
EXPENSES			
Salaries (prorated if less than full-time)			
_____			
_____			
_____			
_____			
_____			
Payroll taxes and benefits (percentage of salaries)			
Bookkeeping contractor			
Other (specify): Total personnel			
Office rent (percentage for program)			
Supplies			
Printing			
Utilities			
Internet/Telephone			
Equipment			
IT			
Copy services			
Postage			
Travel			
Membership dues			
Other (specify): Total nonpersonnel			
Total expenses			

Budget Review Questions

1. Does the budget tell the story of the grant proposal narrative? And is it realistic?

2. Is a budget narrative included that adds further clarification to the numbers and how they are calculated?

3. Does the budget include any in-kind revenues and expenses?

4. Is the percentage of overhead consistent with what the funder has outlined as acceptable in its guidelines?

5. Does the organization have the budget worksheet used to create this proposal budget saved and clearly labeled, so that it has a record of how costs were determined for the expense items?

6. Has there been one final review of the budget to make sure all appropriate expenses and projected revenues are included, and that all calculations are accurate?

7. Have both the executive director and the finance staff person approved it? (If it is a program budget, the lead staffer would be included in the final approval process.)

Now your organization has crafted a budget document that tells in numbers the same story that the proposal tells in words, that provides context in the form a of a budget narrative for any unusual line items, and that includes all appropriate expenses and revenues. It's time to talk about the organization's credentials and how to present them in the Organization Background component of a grant proposal, which is covered in Step 9.

Step 9
Writing the Organizational Background Component

IN ADDITION TO THE PLANNING SECTIONS of the proposal, grantseekers need to develop a clear, concise organization background statement, the purpose of which is to establish a nonprofit's credibility. Using the example from the Alyson Eats proposal, as well as the worksheet for this step, grantseekers will learn how to present their organization's strengths to funders.

Purpose of the Organization Background Statement

What are the mission, values, and other distinguishing characteristics of the organization? And what is it about this organization that enables it to execute on what it promises to deliver? The organization background component answers these questions and more. This proposal section provides credentials for the organization and its ability to fulfill its stated goals and objectives.

Funders may refer to this section as the *organization background* or the *applicant description*, but the same basic information is expected regardless of the title. This component of the proposal should allow the reviewer to get a strong impression that the organization:

- Meets an unmet need or fills an essential role in the community.

- Is fiscally responsible.

- Is well managed.

- Provides important community services.

- Understands the community it serves.

- Reflects that community in its board and staff.

- Has the respect of the community.

Content of the Organization Background Component

Organizations should include the following:

- The history of the organization, including when it was founded.

- The demographics of the community served, followed by the ways in which both the board members and the staff reflect those demographics. This is important information to share, as funders want to ensure that the nonprofit is reflective of the community it seeks to serve.

- Descriptions of innovative programs or special services the organization provides as well as any awards, credentials, and/or special recognition.

The primary goal in crafting this section of the proposal is to establish credibility with potential funders. Organizations should pay attention to what is best to include, given the particular proposal and the funder. The guiding question should be, "What is the key information that this funder needs to know about the organization and its qualifications to solidify the case for support?" For example, when requesting funding for a technical project that makes use of new ways to engage clients online, information about the organization's previous experience in web-based communications, as well as the qualifications of specific staff members who would be responsible for the project, would be critical to reinforcing the nonprofit's capacity to undertake the proposed project. If proposing a collaborative project, thought should be given to using examples of other collaborative projects in which the organization participated, as well as the successful outcomes derived from those collaborations.

Think about the essential components of the organization background and resist the desire to include details that take up valuable space but that do not necessarily add to making the case for an organization. For example, organizations should include a high-level summary of how many board, staff, members (if applicable), and volunteers it has as a part of this proposal component. Supporting documents such as a board roster and staff bios are many times allowed – in fact, required – as appendices to the grant proposal (see Step 11).

If the organization is a start-up, focus on the qualifications of the staff and board to provide grounding and credibility for the start-up endeavor. As a start-up, it is essential to state the unmet needs or unique problem the organization is being created to meet.

Tips for Writing the Organization Background Component

Background Statement

Start with why and when the organization was founded. Its mission statement should be front and center. Next, focus on explaining what the organization does, how it goes about its work, and whom it serves.

This is one of the few sections of a proposal that can be created as a standard component and used repeatedly. Note that grantseekers will be required to make small edits to tailor the background statement for individual funders or to highlight items of special interest to a funder. Otherwise, this section is standard for most proposals.

Here is the organizational background component from Alyson Eats:

Sample Organizational Background Component

Alyson Eats began in 2002 as a joint project of the state university's School of Social Work and the city's Girl Scouts. At the time it was called Feeding Our Neighbors. Every other Friday, the program's volunteers would provide a free, hot meal for hungry or homeless people or anyone who walked in. The dining halls varied as the volunteers were able to secure donated space – a church kitchen one week, a theater basement two weeks later – but they were always so full that volunteers had to turn people away.

It soon became clear that Feeding Our Neighbors, well-meaning as it was, missed the mark in some important ways. The rotating locations made it hard to find; the people providing the service had little input from the people who needed the service regarding how they could make the program more effective and accessible; and Feeding Our Neighbors only functioned during the school year. Despite this, the fact that the dining halls were full to bursting each time revealed just how much hunger there was in Alyson – and that the city needed a much larger and more comprehensive program.

In 2004, Alyson Eats was established as a 501(c)(3) organization, with the help of the state university. The organization has grown from a staff of one to a staff of nine (four full-time and five part-time), with the ability to help ease hunger in numerous ways for thousands of Alyson residents each year. Our board of directors, once composed largely of volunteers from the north side plus a few south-side clergy members, now has most members from the south side who have been personally affected by hunger. Other members of the 12-person board represent our corporate and institutional partners and/or bring specific expertise or resources to the organization. The board is 75 percent people of color. Our executive director grew up hungry in Alyson and is the author of the memoir *Coming Up Empty*.

Using Worksheet 9.1A, the Organization Background Exercise, gather the information for this section of your organization's proposal. See how Alyson Eats used the worksheet in 9.1B.

Next, write the narrative, using the Sample Organization Background Component as a guide. Finally, review the work using the Organization Background Review Questions. Organizations should be able to answer yes to each question.

On the Web

WORKSHEET 9.1A:
Organizational Background Exercise

[Organization Name]

Location

Legal status

Date of founding

Mission statement

Target population

Programs

Partnerships

How unique

Accomplishments

Special recognition

Summary of need statement

Financial

Board and staff

WORKSHEET 9.1B:
Organizational Background Exercise – Alyson Eats

[Organization Name]

Location

South side, city of Alyson

Legal status

501(c)(3)

Date of founding

May 5, 2004

Mission statement

The mission of Alyson Eats is to reduce the suffering of hunger among residents of Alyson's south side.

Target population

130,000 people on Alyson's south side who are experiencing or at risk of hunger

Programs

Eating Is a Right – food pantry and distribution service

Every Youngster Eats – lunches for children during summer

Sharing Is Caring – recruitment of food, donations, volunteers

Food for Life (pilot program) – teaching high school students how to shop for and prepare food

Partnerships

Alyson Clergy Coalition

Alyson High School

Anti-Hunger Coalition

Delta Sigma Theta Sorority

Everybody's Got a Right to Eat

South Side United

State University

WORKSHEET 9.1B:
On the Web **Organizational Background Exercise – Alyson Eats (Continued)**

[Organization Name]

How unique

Oldest and largest food pantry on the south side

Accomplishments

In 2018, distributed 5,500 food boxes totaling 110,000 lbs. of food and 88,000 meals. Made sure 750 children who get school lunches received a free lunch throughout the summer.

Special recognition

Summary of need statement

About 130,000 residents of Alyson, mostly on the south side, are at risk for hunger. On the south side, most children qualify for free lunch at school (76%), and adults sometimes skip meals because there is not enough food in the home (39%).

Financial

2020 budget is $1,352,016. Eighty-five percent already committed: about 57 percent in-kind, 42 percent donations.

Board and staff

Our 12 board members are representative of community we serve, and they are 75 percent people of color.

Four full-time and five part-time staff members. Executive director is African American woman who grew up hungry in Alyson.

Organization Background Review Questions

1. Does the organization background section give the nonprofit credibility by stating its history, qualifications, purpose, programs, target population, total number of people served, and major accomplishments?

2. If developing for a start-up organization or program, does the organization background section highlight the expertise of the individual or individuals leading it?

3. Does the organization background reference prior success and sources of community support for the organization?

4. Does this section highlight any awards received by the organization itself, its leadership, and/or its staff? This can include winning government funding through a competitive process.

Almost all the pieces are now in place. You've developed an idea for the proposal, begun to establish relationships with potential funders, and crafted all the elements of the grant proposal. Only now, close to the end of the proposal development process, is an organization ready to craft what is probably the first and most important element for funders to see: the Proposal Summary, discussed in Step 10.

Step 10
Writing the Proposal Summary

THE PROPOSAL IS NEARLY COMPLETE. Now it is time to produce a brief, crisp summary of the entire proposal. In this step, grantseekers learn the basics of constructing a solid summary. Using the website and the following examples, grantseekers also write a summary for their own proposals.

Purpose and Content of the Summary

A proposal summary (also referred to as an *executive summary*) is a clear, brief abstract of the full proposal. Its purpose is to encapsulate the strongest elements of the grantseeker's proposal, which will then lead the funder to want to read the full proposal. Keep in mind that for some decision-makers at a foundation, the summary may be the *only* part of a proposal they read – so it must contain the essential information a grantmaker needs to know about the organization and its programs.

All proposals of more than five pages in length should contain a summary, and in most cases, funders require a summary as a part of the proposal. Regardless of the length of the proposal, the summary should be no more than one or two pages in length; in many cases the funder's guidelines will specify a length for the summary.

Positioned as the opening element of the proposal, the summary is typically the section written last to ensure that all critical proposal elements are incorporated. A proposal summary should contain the following elements:

- Identification of the applicant (the organization).

- The purpose of the grant.

- The applicant's qualifications to carry out this purpose (the program).

- The anticipated end result.

- The total program or project budget and how much the applicant is requesting from the grantmaker to be used toward that amount.

- The period of time for which the proposal seeks funding (the grant period).

Grantseekers should endeavor to include each of the elements outlined in the previous section in short paragraphs.

A crisp and well-articulated summary helps the funder understand the need for the program, its goals, and its objectives. A good proposal summary paints a picture of the full proposal and entices the funder to read more. Grantseekers should keep in mind that funders receive dozens – and in many cases hundreds – of grant proposals to review during any given funding cycle. A strong summary can help a proposal stand out.

There are many different approaches to employ when writing the proposal summary. Some will start with the compelling problem the program is designed to address, while others will start by introducing the organization, highlighting its reputation and standing, and presenting its overall qualifications. When in doubt, consider following the same order used in the proposal.

If writing the proposal summary is a challenge, know that even the most seasoned grantwriters sometimes struggle with this section because it demands brevity. It requires the writer to encompass the most essential elements of each component of the proposal, in a condensed style – yet in a way that will capture the reader's attention and distinguish this proposal from the rest.

Tips for Writing the Summary

- Decide what the key points are in each section of the proposal's components. Include only those points in the summary.

- Stress the points important to the funder. Make sure the summary highlights the potential funder's priorities.

Study the following executive summary for Alyson Eats. Then complete Worksheet 10.1 to pull together the material for the summary. Finally, review the work by asking the Summary Review Questions. Grantseekers should be able to answer yes to each question.

Sample Summary

Since 2004, Alyson Eats has sought to ease the suffering of some of the approximately 130,000 residents of Alyson who are experiencing or at risk for hunger. Our objective over the coming year is to provide more than 200,000 nutritious meals to hungry children and adults on Alyson's south side. Alyson Eats will engage our four full-time and five part-time staff members, our 50 regular volunteers, and our corporate and other institutional partners across the city to conduct three proven programs to address hunger: our food pantry and distribution service, which will distribute approximately 9,000 boxes of food this year; a summer-time program that will provide meals to about 1,000 children who normally get free lunch at school; and an outreach program to recruit donors of food and funds, as well as volunteers, with a goal this year of recruiting 15 new volunteers and generating 4,500 additional hours of volunteer engagement. We will also pilot a new program to equip teenagers with the skills to eat healthfully and affordably for life, beginning with a class of 30 young people. The Fiscal Year 2020 budget of Alyson Eats is $1,352,016. We appreciate the Future Foundation's consideration of a $50,000 general support grant for the one-year period beginning January 1.

WORKSHEET 10.1:
Summary Questionnaire

1. What is the identity of the organization, and what is its mission?

2. What is the proposed program or project (title, purpose, target population)?

3. Why is the proposed program or project important?

4. What will be accomplished by this program or project during the time period of the grant?

5. Why should the organization be the one to do the program or project (credibility statement)?

6. How much will the program or project cost during the grant time period? How much is being requested from this funder?

Public Funding: Proposal Summary

Many but not all public funding applications may require an executive summary, sometimes called a *proposal abstract*. Keep in mind that, if funded, these statements often become the description of your work in publications and websites. Be sure to stick to character limitations and follow all instructions on exactly what to include.

Helpful Hint

Don't try to write the summary first. Wait until you've finished writing the entire application. When developing an executive summary, you can often start by pulling the first one or two sentences from each section into a paragraph and editing from there. The lead sentences, which you've already written with help from this guide, will introduce the main idea from each section, which you can now edit into a summary of the whole.

Summary Review Questions

1. Does the summary clearly identify the applicant(s)?

2. Does it describe the need to be addressed and the objectives to be achieved?

3. Does it mention the total program or project cost and the amount of funding requested?

4. Is it brief (no more than two pages maximum)?

5. Would a potential funder who read only the summary know the most important points about the organization and its project or program?

Helpful Hint

Be consistent. Now is not the time to introduce new information. Everything in the summary should already be part of the full proposal.

It is now time to assemble the entire proposal package, which is Step 11.

Step 11
Submitting the Application

IN THIS STEP, GRANTSEEKERS LEARN how to submit their application, including attachments. This step takes on a particular significance in light of the seismic shift in the funding world, from paper grant submissions to online submissions via email to online portals for grant submissions.

Most funders have moved to electronic submissions of one kind or another. But there are some that still accept hard copy submissions, including those funders who recognize that there is a digital divide that may make electronic submissions an unfair barrier to organizations that may not have access to high-speed Internet, Adobe, or other technological tools that are essential for online applications. As always, grantseekers should read the funder's requirements for submission and follow them to the letter.

Purpose and Content of the Cover Letter or Email

If an application is being submitted in hard copy, it should be accompanied by a brief cover letter, unless the funder explicitly asks that cover letters not be included. For proposals that are being submitted by email, and not through an online portal, a short cover email is usually in order.

If writing a cover letter, craft a brief, yet informative one that will serve as the first piece of information the funder reads. Keep the details in the proposal and don't take up time with an unnecessarily lengthy cover letter.

- Start the letter with a very brief introduction of the organization and inform the funder of the amount and purpose of the request.
- Use the next paragraph to very briefly highlight the proposal and any salient points.

- The closing paragraph should thank the funder for consideration of the request and should also indicate whom to contact within the organization should the funder have questions. The letter should be signed by the organization's executive director, board president, or both. If the contact person is someone other than the signer(s), be sure to clearly indicate the contact person by name and title, as well as provide that individual's direct email address and phone extension. Grant seekers should take care to minimize confusion by making it as simple as possible for funders to reach the right person in the organization. This final paragraph should also be used to invite a meeting, phone call, or site visit.

Use the following sample cover letter as an example.

Sample Cover Letter

Wendy Wonder
President
Future Foundation
0000 Clinton Avenue, Suite 2330
Anytown, Any State 02009

Dear Ms. Wonder:

On behalf of the board of directors and staff of Alyson Eats, I am honored to submit the following proposal requesting a general operating grant of $50,000. This grant will allow Alyson Eats to address hunger and food insecurity for thousands of vulnerable children and families in our community over the coming year.

Since 2004, Alyson Eats has sought to ease the suffering of some of the approximately 130,000 residents of Alyson who are experiencing or at risk for hunger. Our objective over the coming year is to provide more than 200,000 nutritious meals to hungry children and adults on Alyson's south side through our signature programs. We will also pilot a new program to equip teenagers with the skills to eat healthfully and affordably for life, beginning with a class of 30 young people.

Because of your commitment to addressing safety net and other basic needs in our state, we hope that the Future Foundation will look favorably upon our request for a $50,000 general support grant for the one-year period beginning January 1, 2020. Should you have any questions or need additional information, please contact me directly at (111) 111–1111 or sjones@ae.org. We deeply appreciate your consideration of our request and look forward to hearing from you.

Sincerely,
Shawna Jones
Executive Director

Cover Email

In the case of a cover email, again the grantseeker should keep the communication brief and to the point.

Sample Cover Email

Hello Ms. Wonder. On behalf of Alyson Eats, I am pleased to submit the attached cover sheet, proposal narrative, and required attachments to the Future Foundation for consideration. We are seeking a $50,000 general operating grant for FY 2020.

   We have included the following attachments: grant application cover sheet, proposal narrative, 501(c)(3) letter, FY 2020 operating budget, FY18 audit, board of directors list, and key staff list.

   Should you need anything further or have any questions, please contact me at (111) 111–1111 or sjones@ae.org. We deeply appreciate your consideration of our request and look forward to hearing from you.

Shawna Jones
Executive Director

Purpose and Content of the Appendices or Attachments

Appendices, or attachments, are a necessary and important addition to any grant proposal. These are documents that are not components of the proposal per se, yet they provide valuable information that the funder will need when considering a request. Most funders, regardless of size, and certainly nearly all public funders (local, state, and federal government grants), supply a list of required appendices.

When no list is provided, consider including the following documents:

- The organization's IRS 501(c)(3) tax-exempt status determination letter or fiscal agent's letter, if there is a sponsor, to establish nonprofit status.

- The organization's most recent audited financial statement.

- A list of the organization's board members, their work affiliations, and any other applicable information.

- The organization's overall budget for the current fiscal year.

- The organization's latest annual report (if it prepares an annual report).

In addition to these items, a funder might request profiles of the key staff members assigned to implement or oversee the proposed project or a list of current funders or both. Some funders may also require an attachment section for a letter proposal. Many of the items in the previous list are generally included with these shorter proposals. Letters of Intent, however, will probably require a much-reduced appendices section that includes only the IRS determination letter and possibly a list of members of the board of directors and the organization's budget.

Public Funding Attachments

Public funding applications often have additional requirements for attachments. Please note that some of these attachments the grantseeker must acquire from city, state, or federal government entities, such as a Certificate of Clean Hands or Good Standing, proof of registration with the city or state, and/or a business license.

Online Portal Submissions

Many foundation, corporate, and public funding applications are now submitted through online portals. Although technology is supposed to make the process easier, the truth is that electronic submissions can have technological challenges and the systems can get overloaded when there are a large number of applicants. For that reason:

- Make sure you set up your account in the portal well in advance of the due date. Some portals allow you to sign up instantly; others can take several days.

- For federal grant proposals, you must have a DUNS (Data Universal Numbers System) number, SAM (System for Awards Management) registration, and register for an account with grants.gov. A DUNS number is a unique nine-character number used to identify your organization. The federal government uses the DUNS number to track how federal money is allocated. SAM is a web-based, government-wide application that collects, validates, stores, and disseminates business information about the federal government's trading partners in support of the contract awards, grants, and electronic payment processes. For information on all of these registrations, visit grants.gov.

- Be sure to double-check whether the portal is one that will allow applicants to save submissions in progress, or whether the full submission must be completed in one sitting. This distinction is critical, as one allows grantseekers to edit as they go, save their work, and come back to complete the submission. The other does not allow this functionality and will require a dedicated amount of time and attention to detail to complete in one sitting. If the portal does not save-as-you-go, complete the narrative in a Word document you can save, and then cut and paste the answers.

- Find time to upload attachments well before the deadline. This can be a time-consuming process in certain systems.

- Take care to submit electronic proposals sooner rather than closer to the deadline date. *Always keep in mind that technology is known to pick the most inopportune moments to fail.*

Use the checklist in Worksheet 11.1 to make sure the proposal is complete and ready to submit.

Emailing the Proposal

A simple, clutter-free, and neatly packaged proposal creates the perception of a well-organized, successful organization. This holds true for an email proposal submission. When submitting via email, grantseekers should always convert the proposal and attachments to PDF (portable document format), which makes documents present more professionally and prevents the documents from being edited by locking formatting in place. As a general rule, organizations should never submit documents electronically that are not in PDF format, unless the funder specifically asks for documents in another format. Also *be sure to check for any file naming requirements* the funder may have.

When emailing the proposal:

- Double-check the name and email address of all required recipients.

- Check the requirements for the subject line. Some funders ask for a specific text here, such as "AlysonEatsApplication-1–1–2020."

- Make sure all attachments are in PDF format unless otherwise instructed by the funder. As noted earlier, check for any file-naming requirements.

- List all the attachments that are included with the email.

- Include a contact person's email address.

- Check the cc line to ensure anyone who needs to be included on the email is there. However, don't cc a big group of people from your organization. You can forward a copy to those who need to be informed that the email has been sent.

Paper Proposal Submissions

If the funder is requesting a paper submission, or if you are submitting by paper by choice and it is allowable by the funder, carefully read the funder's guidelines to confirm the number of proposal copies that should be submitted. Funders might request an original and several copies of a full proposal, so make sure to follow their instructions. If more than one copy of the proposal is requested, clearly mark which proposal is the original. Organizations should also be prepared for requests to submit proposals on a thumb drive along with a paper copy.

In an effort to cut down on use of paper products in general, proposals (other than letter proposals with only a few appendices) should be neatly arranged and held together with a large binder clip, rather than a folder. Start with the full proposal, the budget, and then the appendices in the order listed in the guidelines. Leave the cover letter outside the binder clip for the original proposal only. Each copy of the proposal can be fully binder-clipped, with the cover letter copy inside the clip. Grantseekers can paperclip each section of the proposal if desired (narrative proposal, budget, appendices), as that might make accessing the proposal overall easier for the funder.

Placing a proposal in a three-ring notebook, having it spiral-bound, or spending unnecessary money to have it color copied does not add value. Presentation is important, but only from a neatness and orderliness standpoint.

Helpful Hint

Before submitting a proposal, take some time for these final quality-control checks.

- Proofread the proposal and cover letter. This should be done by someone *other* than the proposal writer.

- Look for leftovers. If you are reusing some text from a previous proposal (which is perfectly fine to do), such as the description of your organization, make sure the previous funder's name does not appear anywhere in the current proposal. Use the search function to find every time the word *foundation* appears, and confirm that the proper funder is named.

- Review the grant guidelines to make sure you have provided all the materials requested, in the order and formats requested.

Reality Check

After submitting the proposal, send a copy to the people who will be responsible for carrying out the work the proposal describes, such as other staff members in your organization and partners. A grant is an investment from a funder in your organization or program; it is also a commitment from your organization or program to the funder that you will complete the work described in the proposal. That commitment does not rest with the proposal writer, but with the people who will lead the funded activities (unless, of course, the proposal writer *is* the program leader).

Now it's time to develop an appropriate follow-up strategy, based on your relationship with the funder and funder guidelines on contacting them about pending proposals, which is discussed in the next chapter. Step 12 suggests some strategies for maintaining contact with those funders and moving the proposal through their grantmaking process.

Step 12
Sustaining Relationships with Funders

TIME TO TAKE INVENTORY: a solid program plan addressing a compelling community problem was completed. A substantive grant proposal employing the steps outlined in this workbook was developed. The proposal was successfully submitted following the funder's grant guidelines. Time to celebrate? Well ... not just yet.

Following Up on the Proposal

Most funders provide detailed grant guidelines, inclusive of deadline dates, for their grantmaking process. Also included will be the amount of time that the funder requires to review all proposals. Pay attention to whether the funder requests that organizations not call during a specific period, as this is a request that should be honored.

Also, be aware that some funders incorporate site visits into the grant making process, and they want to save all discussion and questions for that time. For funders with online grant proposal submission processes – which is now the majority using either email or portal – grantseekers are likely to receive an e-notification of some sort that will confirm receipt.

Managing a Site Visit

A site visit occurs when the funder comes to the organization's site (or the site of the proposed program) to visit with leaders, staff, board members, and those the organization serves. Site visits are not a part of every foundation's review process, and those foundations that include site visits do not request them of every organization. Typically, if a site visit is requested, it is as part of a vetting process for a proposal in the advanced stages of consideration. It is important to note that a site visit is not a guarantee of funding; however, it does signal a strong connection between the foundation, the organization, and the proposed program.

When a site visit is requested, the key staff assigned to the program are essential to the process because they are the people who created the program plan, and they are the ones who will be responsible for the hands-on implementation of the project. They should be present during the visit, as should the executive director and the person who can answer financial or budgetary questions. If the program targets a specific group of people, representation in the form of one or more individuals from the population to be served or engaged is always welcome, as they can provide the most useful testimony for the program, its significance, and its power for change.

If a nonprofit is selected for a site visit, use the following to-do list to prepare:

- Confirm the participation of all key people involved with the program.

- Send the full proposal to everyone participating, and request that they (re)familiarize themselves with it.

- If the funder has provided questions in advance of the site visit, share those with all site visit participants.

- Meet with everyone in advance of the actual site visit to ensure that everyone is on the same page in terms of knowledge about the program and its goals, objectives, and strategies, and that everyone understands who will be answering which questions as well as who is moderating the visit.

If the funder requests a tour, decide on what the important elements are for the funder's representatives to see, and plan the tour in advance. As before, inform everyone who will be a part of it of the date, time, objectives, and logistics of the tour. Make sure everything is in order and try to schedule the tour for a time when funders can see the organization in action; and check with staff to make sure it won't be disruptive to have visitors and/or violate clients' confidentiality or privacy in any way.

Responding to the Funder's Decision

Funding decisions are typically delivered via email, though there are times when a call is made. If the organization's proposal resulted in a winning grant, it is definitely a reason to celebrate. If the organization's proposal is declined, it can be a real disappointment. In both cases, grantseekers need to continue with their relationship building.

When the Proposal Is Funded

Winning a grant is a great feeling of accomplishment, and a great relief because it means confirmed resources for an important purpose. There is nothing like getting that call, letter, or email announcing that the grant is being awarded. A thank-you email to the funder is certainly in order as soon as word is received regarding the request being approved. As busy as funders are, hearing from grantees about how the programs – and organizations – they've funded are progressing is generally welcomed with enthusiasm. In most foundations with paid staff, the grantmaking process requires staff to advocate for the programs they recommend for funding. Consider them partners and keep them apprised on a quarterly basis (minimum) with a brief note, an email, a call, a personalized newsletter, or whatever form of communication is most effective and appropriate.

Following an email to the funder, which should happen within the same day as notification, a formal letter of thanks should also be sent to the funder and signed by the executive director.

Most funders anticipate some sort of public recognition of its grants. Standard forms of recognition include a feature in the grantee's newsletter and inclusion on a donor list on the recipient's website or in the annual report. Consider the level of recognition in proportion to the amount of funds received; that should guide the selection process for the appropriate recognition level. A large grant may warrant special recognition at an organization's annual event or ceremony of some sort, or a media announcement. Ultimately, if anything beyond a newsletter mention and inclusion in a donor list is being considered, it should be discussed with the funder in advance of making any decisions. Organizations should not make any assumptions about funder recognition, particularly if the grant award letter does not provide specific guidance on the subject.

If the funding institution (or the grant) is to remain anonymous, the funder will clearly stipulate that fact in its grant award letter. In such situations, the funder's name should not be mentioned anywhere publicly, and care should be taken in all internal records to mark the grantmaker as anonymous.

When a grant is awarded, the nonprofit will:

- Receive initial notification of the award. This primarily happens via email, though some still notify via phone call or letter.
- Receive official confirmation in the form of a Grant Agreement Letter. Again, most grant agreements are sent electronically, but you should continue to pay attention to your regular mail.

- Have the organization's executive director and other appropriate staff (such as the person responsible for program implementation and the person responsible for organization finances) review the Grant Agreement Letter to ensure that the nonprofit will be able to comply with all its stipulations, as it is a legally binding agreement.

- Return the signed Grant Agreement Letter within three to five days of receipt.

- Provide quarterly, semiyearly, and/or yearly progress reports. Each funder has different requirements, but these will be spelled out clearly in the Grant Agreement Letter. Timely reports are especially critical if the nonprofit hopes to be eligible to reapply to this funder for further support.

Notify the funder of all major changes or issues identified in the program as soon as possible. Staffing changes, a strategy that is not working, and participant recruitment that is well below what was originally targeted are all examples of situations about which your funding partner should be informed.

When the Proposal Is Not Funded

For every organization that wins a grant, dozens – sometimes hundreds – of organizations will receive declination letters. On average, a typical foundation can make grants in response to approximately 10–20 percent of the total requests it receives in every funding cycle. Sometimes the approval rate is even smaller.

An organization's declination letter is likely to be very general and provide vague reasons for the denial. So grantseekers should consider following up with the funder via email to see if any additional feedback can be shared about why the organization's proposal was not funded. Consider asking the following three questions:

1. Were there any parts of the funder's guidelines that were missed? (Find out up front if the proposal was disqualified for any reason.)

2. Was additional information or further clarity needed in the program plan or grant proposal to make it more competitive?

3. Is it recommended that the organization resubmit a proposal for this program at another time? If so, when?

Be sure to thank the funder for considering the request. Let civility be the rule and remember that there is always the next cycle.

The reality is this: there are many stellar programs that do not get funded. There are compelling grant proposals that do not get funded.

The demand for foundation and corporate (and government) grants is simply too high, and competition for these dollars grows more challenging each year.

Grantseekers should be on a mission to be organized, truthful, respectful, consistent, and persistent in their grantseeking endeavors. Keep in mind that a denial from a funder does not mean a program lacks merit, nor does it mean that a program will never get funded.

Continue building funder relationships. Consider keeping all the funders identified as a match for the organization's programs on the organization's mailing list; also invite them to events and continue to share organization successes with them via periodic updates through emails and other communications.

A note about public funding: Many public funders will provide applicants – those who are successful as well as those who aren't – with detailed information about their application, including the proposal score and reviewer comments. This information can be invaluable in developing and improving future applications.

Final Thoughts

The primary goal of *Winning Grants Step by Step, Fifth Edition* is to provide time-tested, nuts and bolts guidance for proposal development and a framework for how the steps should come together. A secondary goal is to provide some additional context for the grantseeking process itself. A well-written, well-organized grant proposal is a critical component of the funding equation, but there is more to do to ultimately "win" that grant.

Providing organizations with the knowledge that grantseeking is a process that in many cases spans months – and in some cases, years – of cultivation and relationship building is an important piece of the funding equation. Finally, what most differentiates this edition from the previous ones is the undeniable role technology now plays in the "winning grants" process. From prospect research to proposal submission to the actual grant award itself, which may come in the form of a wire transfer directly into the organization's bank account rather than a paper check, there is no denying the increasing influence of technology in the grantseeking process.

Resource A—Sample Proposal

ALYSON EATS
General Support Proposal to the
FUTURE FOUNDATION
October 1, 2019

Introduction

Almost one million people live in the city of Alyson. Every night, some 130,000 of them are at risk of going to bed hungry. The city is roughly split into two regions that might as well be two different worlds: the north side, which is largely composed of people who are white, middle-class or affluent; and the south side, which is home primarily to people of color who are working-class or poor.

Whereas the north side has a larger population, the south side has a younger population, more families with children, and more people who lack consistent, reliable, and affordable access to nutritious food. Officially, this lack is known as food insecurity. To hungry families, it is known as suffering. Easing this suffering has been the mission of Alyson Eats since our founding in 2004.

We ask the Future Foundation to support our efforts with a general support grant of $50,000 for Fiscal 2020 (January 1–December 31, 2020). Our organizational goals closely align with the Foundation's mission to build a better future for families struggling with poverty in our state.

Executive Summary

Since 2004, Alyson Eats has sought to ease the suffering of some of the approximately 130,000 residents of Alyson who are experiencing or at risk for hunger. Our objective over the coming year is to provide more than 200,000 nutritious meals to hungry children and adults on Alyson's south side. Alyson Eats will engage our four full-time and five part-time staff members, our 50 regular volunteers, and our corporate and other institutional partners across the city to conduct three proven programs to address hunger: our food pantry and distribution service, which will distribute approximately 9,000 boxes of food this year; a summer-time program that will provide meals to about 1,000 children who normally get free lunch at school; and an outreach program to recruit donors of food and funds, as well as volunteers, with a goal this year of recruiting 15 new volunteers and generating 4,500 additional hours of volunteer engagement. We will also pilot a new program to equip teenagers with the skills to eat healthfully and affordably for life, beginning with a class of 30 young people. The Fiscal Year 2020 budget of Alyson Eats is $1,352,016. We appreciate the Future Foundation's consideration of a $50,000 general support grant for the one-year period beginning January 1.

Organization Background

Alyson Eats began in 2002 as a joint project of the state university's School of Social Work and the city's Girl Scouts. At the time, it was called Feeding Our Neighbors. Every other Friday, the program's volunteers would provide a free, hot meal for hungry or homeless people or anyone who walked in. The dining halls varied as the volunteers were able to secure donated space – a church kitchen one week, a theater basement two weeks later – but they were always so full that volunteers had to turn people away.

It soon became clear that Feeding Our Neighbors, well-meaning as it was, missed the mark in some important ways. The rotating locations made it hard to find; the people providing the service had little input from the people who needed the service regarding how they could make the program more effective and accessible; and Feeding Our Neighbors only functioned during the school year. Despite this, the fact that the dining halls were full to bursting each time revealed just how much hunger there was in Alyson – and that the city needed a much larger and more comprehensive program.

In 2004, Alyson Eats was established as a 501(c)(3) organization, with the help of the state university. The organization has grown from a staff of one to a staff of nine (four full-time and five part-time), with the ability to help ease hunger in numerous ways for thousands of Alyson residents each year. Our board of directors, once composed largely of volunteers from the north side plus a few south-side clergy members, now has a majority of members from the south side who have been personally affected by hunger. Other members of the 12-person board represent our corporate and institutional partners and/or bring specific expertise or resources to the organization. The board is 75 percent people of color. Our executive director grew up hungry in Alyson, and is the author of the memoir *Coming Up Empty*.

Problem Statement

Approximately 130,000 residents of Alyson, most of them living on the city's south side, are at risk for hunger. On the south side, most children qualify for free lunch at school (76%). Adults sometimes skip meals because there is not enough food in the home (39%), and many parents worry at the beginning of the month how they will feed their children by the end of the month (45%), as a survey conducted last year by the Alyson City Council revealed. The summer months are particularly difficult because schools, and school lunch programs, are closed.

Convenience stores, take-out places, and fast-food restaurants abound on the south side, and many families must make do with the food they offer. Fresh, nutritious food is not only more expensive than less-nutritious food ($1.50 a day costlier, according to researchers at the Harvard School of Public Health),[1] but also geographically out of reach for most residents of the south side, a large proportion of whom do not own cars. Only one-third of the neighborhoods in the south side are within reasonable distance – less than three miles – of a full-service grocery store via public transit. As a result, many south-side children grow up rarely having been in a supermarket, and with no opportunity to learn the consumer skills that can enable them to choose and afford healthful food throughout their lives.

We know that hunger is not merely the lack of food; it is the lack of access to resources, economic opportunity, and social mobility – in other words, poverty. Although Alyson Eats supports and partners with organizations that fight the root causes of poverty, including several grantees of the Future Foundation, our goal is more immediate: to reduce the suffering of those who are hungry. To this end we conduct a number of programs that serve and involve the low-income residents of Alyson's south side.

Goals and Objectives

The goal of Alyson Eats is to reduce hunger in our city. Our objective over the coming year is to provide more than 200,000 nutritious meals to children and adults in Alyson who are experiencing or at risk for hunger. Alyson Eats will engage our staff members, our 50 regular volunteers, and our partners in corporations and institutions across the city to conduct three proven programs to address hunger; and we will pilot a new program this year to equip teenagers with the skills to eat healthfully and affordably for life. Each of these programs has its own goals and objectives.

Strategies

Alyson Eats provides most of our antihunger services through our three core programs, which we have tested and refined over the years and adapted to meet the changing needs of our communities.

Eating Is a Right (EAR)

Alyson Eats created a large food pantry in a warehouse on the south side. Here we receive, inspect, organize and distribute boxes of healthful groceries for hungry families. The pantry is open for pick-up Wednesday through Sunday, from 6:00 a.m.–8:00 p.m. year-round to enable both day- and nightshift workers to stop in. Through the EAR program, we also distribute food boxes to central locations throughout the city, including schools, parks, churches/mosques/synagogues, and the main bus station. EAR is our oldest and most substantial program, requiring an extensive team of staff and volunteers in the warehouse, pantry, and behind the scenes, to source, inspect, transport, categorize, and distribute the food. As one tiny but vital example, we need a small army of volunteers—usually students—to fold and set up hundreds of cardboard boxes, which we buy in flat-packed bundles.

In 2020 we will distribute at least 9,000 boxes of nutritious food, each box weighing about 20 pounds and sufficient for 16 meals. This will total approximately 144,000 meals and 180,000 pounds of food during 2020. We do not ask for or keep track of our clients' names, but we estimate that the 9,000 food boxes will serve at least 3,000 households, since many of our clients are "repeat customers" who come in a few times a year for food supplies.

Goal: To provide access to 144,000 healthful meals for individuals and families in Alyson's south side.

Objective: The distribution of 180,000 pounds of nutritious food will reduce the risk of hunger for at least 3,000 households.

Every Youngster Eats (EYE)

During the summer months, Alyson Eats distributes ready-made lunches to childcare centers, nonprofit day camps, and so forth to make up for the free school lunches that children rely on during the school year. We partner with a local organization that helps parents organize childcare collectives, to make sure independent childcare providers have access to the EYE program's meals for the children they care for.

Goal: To reduce the summer school-lunch gap for 1,000 children.

Objective: 1,000 children will receive lunch five days a week from June through August (12 weeks), for a total of 60,000 meals.

Sharing Is Caring

This is our outreach program, through which we recruit and engage individuals, institutions, and businesses from across the city to participate in our antihunger activities. Our staff, volunteers, and board members seek to enroll businesses, grocery stores, caterers, and so forth to provide fresh, unopened goods to the EAR and EYE programs. We also help schools, congregations, Scout troops and others to organize food drives.

Sharing Is Caring is also the program through which we recruit and train a large portion of our volunteers. In many cases, these are people who work for the businesses and institutions that share their fresh food with us. We also recruit at schools, houses of worship, and through African-American sororities, whose alumnae are among our strongest volunteer leaders. Every new volunteer goes through a three-hour training program and is assigned an experienced volunteer as a mentor. Each volunteer is asked to give at least 25 hours a month (e.g., one shift per week at the food pantry). We provide ongoing training, leadership development, and education opportunities for volunteers so they can understand more deeply the causes of hunger and poverty and the power of informed citizens to change these dynamics. Although our staff members lead some of these programs, many of our training and teaching programs are led by seasoned volunteers who have taken on important leadership roles. In 2020 we will recruit 40 additional volunteers, with the expectation that most volunteers will drop off or participate occasionally, but that we will be able to retain and develop 15 core volunteers from the group.

Goal: To increase volunteer engagement and participation by 30 percent.

Objective: 15 new core volunteers will contribute 4,500 hours of volunteer service.

Food for Life

This is a new program that we will test in 2020. The program is designed to help teenagers learn how to shop for and prepare simple, inexpensive, healthful meals from scratch, using widely available and/or seasonal ingredients. Of course, many young people in Alyson learn this from their own family members. Food for Life is for teenagers who don't have access to such experiences, such as the many south-side kids whose parents work two and three jobs.

During this first year, we will take three teams of 10 young people each on field trips to supermarkets and farmers markets, to familiarize them with the food products available in the wider world above 38th Street, and get them comfortable navigating the process of grocery shopping. We'll teach the young people skills such as how to read food labels, compare prices, and shop for sales, as well as basic cooking techniques. At the end of the year, students will invite their families to the Alyson Eats offices to enjoy a meal they themselves have shopped for and prepared.

But as we mentioned earlier in this proposal, *widely available* does not necessarily apply to Alyson residents who live in what is essentially a food desert, and seasonal produce may not be something they regularly encounter. A longer-term goal of Food for Life (beyond this one-year grant period) is to encourage local farmers markets both to establish more markets in the south side and to accept SNAP payments. Ultimately, we hope to introduce young people to an array of food choices that may be available to them in the near future, if not already, and to introduce food sellers to a whole new customer base they are not currently reaching.

Goal: To test the efficacy of a pilot program in improving eating habits and consumer awareness among high school students.

Objective: Thirty high school students enrolled in the pilot program will complete a pre- and post-assessment of the program's first year and discussion of how to refine the program in future years.

Evaluation

Our three core programs have specific annual goals, objectives, and outcomes to achieve during 2020:

- The EAR program seeks to provide 144,000 nutritious meals totaling 180,000 pounds of food for individuals and families in Alyson's south side.

- The EYE program aims to provide lunch five days a week to 1,000 children over the summer, for a total of 60,000 meals.

- The Sharing Is Caring program strives to recruit 15 new volunteers in order to increase volunteer engagement by 30 percent.

Because we have been conducting these programs for more than a decade, we've established a rigorous system of quarterly check-ins to track our progress toward the annual goals.

In addition to these quantifiable benchmarks, Alyson Eats regularly seeks input from our partners, volunteers, and the people we serve. These inputs range from quarterly conversations in which volunteers and staff are invited to talk about what they think is working well and what could be improved, to a series of poster boards we display on the walls of our food pantry that enable our clients to tell us, through the use of colored stick-on dots, how they think we're doing and what we could do better. Thanks to our historical and current partnership with the university, particularly the School of Social Work, students frequently work with Alyson Eats to create evaluation instruments and conduct assessments of our programs as part of their field practice. We take all these evaluations seriously, and continually refine our programs to meet the needs and standards the assessments reveal.

Despite this experience, we will need additional help in determining how best to assess the effectiveness of our new Food for Life program. If we are fortunate enough to receive a grant from the Future Foundation, we would use some of the funds to contract with a professional evaluator to help us establish a strong baseline and benchmarks.

Sustainability

Nothing would please Alyson Eats more than to go out of business because there's no longer a need for our services. Short of that, we have a robust fundraising operation.

Our budget for 2020 is $1.3 million. We have commitments totaling 85 percent of this amount. Of our current commitments, approximately 57 percent are in-kind donations of volunteer work, food and facilities; 42 percent are donations from individuals, including our volunteers and their friends, and from institutions and foundations. With few exceptions, these are local and regional funders like the Future Foundation. We take it as a vote of confidence that the people who see our work close-up are the ones most moved to invest in our ongoing efforts. In the past few years, a new population of individual donors has emerged: people who once relied on our services, and now are on firm enough footing economically that they can turn around and donate to our programs. Although we value and appreciate every donation, the gifts from former clients mean the most to us.

Alyson Eats has yet to raise $197,016, which represents about 15 percent of our 2020 budget. A grant at the requested level from the Future Foundation would reduce our revenue gap by approximately 25 percent.

Conclusion

Alyson Eats is grateful for this opportunity to seek support from the Future Foundation. We hope you will consider a general support grant of $50,000 for the one-year period beginning January 1, 2020. A budget is attached.

Alyson Eats Fiscal Year 2020 Operating Budget	
Revenues	**Projected**
GS support from foundations (Open Communities Fund; Southside Community Foundation; Jane Irving Family Foundation; individual donors)	$250,000
Restricted/Programmatic support	$225,000
Abundant Living Community Church	$10,000
Membership and T-shirt sales	$10,000
Facilities costs – in-kind*	$10,000
Volunteers* – 50 x $500 mo. Each average (in-kind support)	$300,000
In-kind food donations*	$350,000
Revenue Subtotal	**$1,155,000**
Expenses	**Projected**
Staffing & Fringe (28%) for nine permanent staff (one manager, three full-time program, five half-time)	$391,680
Facilities (in-kind)	$10,000
Board support and D&O Insurance	$10,000
Volunteer support (in-kind)	$300,000
Food and Supplies—purchase	$150,000
Food and Supplies (in-kind)	$350,000
Programmatic supplies, technology, and marketing materials	$20,000
Evaluation	$5,000
Indirect expenses	$115,336
Expense Subtotal	**$1,352,016**
Alyson Eats FY2020 Operating Budget – Revenue Gap as of October 1, 2019: $197,016	

*Represents in-kind donations, rather than cash.

Note

1. Press release, Harvard School of Public Health, December 5, 2013, https://www.hsph.harvard.edu/news/press-releases/healthy-vs-unhealthy-diet-costs-1–50-more/.

Resource B—How to Research Funders

ORGANIZATIONS NEED TO CONDUCT effective prospect research to identify funding institutions that best match the organization's mission and programs. The most up-to-date, robust resources for all kinds of funding – foundations and governmental – can be found online.

The Foundation Center (http://foundationcenter.org) is rich with information and is the primary source of information on the field of philanthropy. It is a nonprofit organization itself, established back in 1956, and it maintains a comprehensive database on foundations, which can be accessed through its website, its five regional hubs, and its network of more than 400 funding information centers located in public libraries, community foundations, and educational institutions around the world.

The Foundation Center provides some of the more basic foundation information for free, including each private foundation's IRS Form 990-PF. This form, which assesses compliance with the Internal Revenue Code, lists the organization's assets, receipts, expenditures, and compensation of directors and officers, and it lists grants awarded during the previous year. There are many ways to access a foundation's 990-PF including:

990 Finder (http://foundationcenter.org/find-funding/990-finder)

Foundation Director Online Quick Start (http://foundationcenter.org/find-funding/fdo-quick-start)

GuideStar (www.guidestar.org)

Economic Research Institute (www.erieri.com)

Pro Publica (https://projects.propublica.org/nonprofits/)

Note that this information is merely baseline data that will provide the following: contact information, type of foundation, IRS exemption status, financial data, and employer identification number (EIN).

Accessing the more comprehensive data such as previous grants, annual report information, and board and staff leadership is available for a fee through a Foundation Center resource, the Foundation Directory Online (http://fconline.fdncenter.org), which offer more comprehensive, in-depth information available on U.S. grantmakers and their grants.

Another option is to go directly to the source, which is each foundation's individual website. Most foundations have websites containing extensive information about its leadership, theory of change, funding areas, previous grantees, and – in most instances – its grant guidelines.

Grant Space (grantspace.org), a project of the Foundation Center, offers a free tutorial for getting started in grantseeking. They also offer a resource for those seeking scholarships, fellowships and awards at gtionline.foundationcenter.org.

Philanthropy News Digest, also a project of the Foundation Center, offers a resource of available Requests for Proposals (RFP) for various funding opportunities (http://philanthropynewsdigest.org/rfp).

As for public funding, here are some of the better resources to get started:

Assistance Listings (formerly Catalogue of Federal Domestic Assistance) – A running list of all available public funding from the federal government and includes live links to each official Request for Proposal grant guidelines. (https://beta.sam.gov/search?index=cfda)

GRANTS.GOV – It is currently the single access point for over 900 grant programs offered by the 26 federal grantmaking agencies, allowing organizations to electronically find and apply for competitive grant opportunities. A downloadable app is available from this site. (https://www.grants.gov/web/grants)

National Institutes of Health—The largest funder of biomedical research in the world, NIH funds research in just about every area that's remotely related to human health and disease. (http://grants.nih.gov/grants.oer .htm)

National Science Foundation – An independent federal agency, the U.S. National Science Foundation funds approximately 20 percent of all federally supported basic research conducted at America's colleges and universities. www.nsf.gov/funding

Community of Science – Community of Science claims the "largest, most comprehensive database of available funding," with 700 member institutions. Individuals can register for free, but this won't get you access to the funding database. http://pivot.cos.com

Whether focused on foundation grants, individual scholarships, or government public funding, prospect research, when done correctly, should lead to the following:

- The identification of prospect foundations, corporations, and public funding opportunities – those whose interests most closely match what the organization is seeking.

- A comprehensive understanding of the specific interests of each prospect to better target each proposal accordingly.

- The identification of any connections between the organization and one or more prospect funders; the connection might be through someone who is on the organization's board of directors or staff or who is a volunteer or donor.

Here are some steps to online funder research:

1. Identify the search criteria to be used in advance of starting the research. These can include key words, subject matter, geographic area, target audience, gender, race and ethnicity, and any other criteria that fit the organization's interests. Doing this in advance will help grantseekers refine and target the research.

2. Determine the subject areas and type of support indexes (new program, capital, general operating, and so on). Those funders that fund within the type of support being sought and that also express an interest in one or more of the subject areas are likely to be the strongest prospects. Keep an eye out for funders located in the organization's geographic area, as they are the ones most likely to consider the grantseeker's proposal.

3. Study the information on each prospect identified to learn everything possible about it, because this will allow the grantseeker to further determine whether there is truly a match.

4. Once funding sources that best match the organization's funding needs are identified, visit the foundations' websites and get to know them even more. Review their annual reports, success stories of previous grants made, staff biographies, and everything else they are sharing with the public. Visiting each prospect funder's website to check guidelines is also a critical step because guidelines do change over time – and sometimes the changes are significant – but the changes may not have made their way yet into the online directory.

5. With all the information obtained from prospect funder websites, get a much clearer sense of how to target the proposals to "speak" to each funder in a language to which its program officer is likely to relate. Grantseekers will also have a grasp on how much they can reasonably request from each funder.

6. It is strongly advised that grantseekers employ a prospect grid that lists every prospect identified; the organization's program that most closely aligns with each prospect's funding interests as outlined in its grant guidelines; the proposed request amount; deadline dates; and all other pertinent information. There are several online tools and spreadsheet software that can be used for this purpose. Share the prospect list with the organization's board and staff to determine whether anyone has a personal contact on the board or staff of any of these prospect funders.

Here are a few additional, more creative, ways to identify funder prospects:

1. Visit the websites of nonprofit organizations that are similar in their mission, geographic area, or target audience and review their donor pages. What foundations support these other organizations? Once those foundations are identified, look up the websites of these foundations to find out more about these potential funders.

2. Grantees should survey their surroundings. Are there any corporate headquarters close by? Or maybe franchise outlets of popular chains (of restaurants, retail stores, conveniences stores, and the like)? Contact their corporate headquarters and find out about their corporate contribution programs – for both funding grants and in-kind support.

3. Look on the donor walls of the local hospitals, universities, and museums. Make note of the foundations and corporations that support these institutions, and then look them up online to find out more. Who knows? Grantseekers just might find a match, especially if the organization is of the same type.

4. Go to the Forum of Regional Associations of Grantmakers (www .givingforum.org) to locate the local regional association of grantmakers, and then visit that local association's website to see what resources and leads it might provide.

5. See whether a meeting can be set up with the donor-relations staff person at the local community foundation. The goal is to find out more about the donor-advised funds at the community foundation and see if there are funds where the donor advisors' interests potentially match the grantseeker's programs.

Resource C— Resources for Grantseekers

Advancing Human Rights http://humanrightsfunding.org/

Forum of Regional Associations of Grantmakers www.givingforum.org

Foundation Search America www.foundationsearch.com

Funders Online www.fundersonline.org

Fundsnet Services Online www.fundsnetservices.com

Give Spot www.givespot.com/resources/grantseekers.htm

Grant Advisor Plus www.grantadvisor.com/

Grant Spy www.grantspy.com/resources.php

Grant Station https://grantstation.com/

The Grantsmanship Center www.tgci.com

Resources for Individual Grantseekers

Foundation Center: Links for Individual Grant seekers http:// foundationcenter.org/getstarted/individuals/

Grant Space: Resources for Individual Grant seekers http://grantspace .org/Tools/Knowledge-Base/Individual-Grantseekers

National Scholarship Funders Association https://www .scholarshipproviders.org/page/SchSeekerResources/Scholarship- Seeker-Resources.htm

Prospect Research Tools

DonorSearch http://donorsearch.net/

The Foundation Center: Find Funders http://foundationcenter.org/findfunders/

GuideStar www.guidestar.org

Logic Models

Centers for Disease Control: Identifying the Components of a Logic Model https://www.cdc.gov/std/program/pupestd/components%20of%20a%20logic%20model.pdf

Free Management Library https://managementhelp.org/evaluation/logic-model-guide.htm#overview

Child Welfare Information Gateway: Evaluation Toolkit and Logic Model www.childwelfare.gov/preventing/evaluating/tookit.cfm

Community Tool Box https://ctb.ku.edu/en/table-of-contents/overview/models-for-community-health-and-development/logic-model-development/example

Corporation for National & Community Service https://www.nationalservice.gov/sites/default/files/upload/OpAC%20Logic%20Model%20draft%20in%20progress.pdf

Innovation Network: Point K—Tell Me More www.innonet.org/?section_id=64&content_id=185

Nonprofit Webinars: A Guide to Logic Models http://nonprofitwebinars.com/past_webinars/10122011-a-guide-to-logic-models-grant-writing/

Theory of Change www.theoryofchange.org

Measuring Social Change, Social Justice

The Center for Effective Philanthropy: Assessment and Social Justice Funding www.effectivephilanthropy.org/blog/2010/05/assessment-and-social-justice-funding/

Innovation Network: Measuring Social Change, Lessons from the Field www.innonet.org/index.php?section_id=6&content_id=592

Social Edge: A Program of the Skoll Foundation www.socialedge.org/discussions/success-metrics/measuring-social-impact/

Program Evaluation

Delaware Association of Nonprofits www.delawarenonprofit.org/ infocentral/programeval.php

Florida Atlantic University: Nonprofit Resource Center http://wise.fau .edu/~rcnyhan/images/program.html

Free Management Library: Basic Guide to Program Evaluation (Including Outcomes Evaluation) http://managementhelp.org/evaluation/ program-evaluation-guide.htm

GrantSpace: Knowledge Base http://grantspace.org/Tools/Knowledge-Base/Grantmakers/Program-evaluation

The James Irvine Foundation: Evaluation. http://irvine.org/evaluation/ tools-and-resources

Budget Information

The Charles Stewart Mott Foundation www.mott.org/ grantsandguidelines/ForGrantees/accounting/indirectvsdirect

Nonprofit Accounting Basics: Reporting and Operations www .nonprofitaccountingbasics.org/reporting-operations/budgeting-terms-concepts

Small Business Chron: How to Calculate Overhead for a Nonprofit http:// smallbusiness.chron.com/calculate-overhead-nonprofit-13808.html

Government Grant Opportunities

Catalog of Federal Domestic Assistance http://12.46.245.173/cfda/cfda .html

Grants.gov www.grants.gov

National Endowment for the Arts www.arts.endow.gov

USA.gov for Nonprofits www.usa.gov/Business/Nonprofit.shtml

U.S. Department of Education (ED) www.ed.gov/fund/landing.jhtml

U.S. Department of Housing and Urban Development (HUD) www.hud .gov/grants/index.cfm

Board Resources

BoardSource. www.boardsource.org

The Board Resource Center. www.brcenter.org

Charity Strong. https://www.charitystrong.org/page/Resources

National Council of Nonprofits. www.councilofnonprofits.org

Nonprofit Board Resource Center. https://www.bridgespan.org/
    insights/library/boards/nonprofit-board-resource-center

Research and Data Resources

Center on Budget and Policy Priorities www.cbpp.org/

Economic Policy Institute www.epi.org

National Center for Charitable Statistics http://nccs.urban.org

The Opportunity Agenda http://opportunityagenda.org/

The Urban Institute www.urban.org

Violence Policy Center www.vpc.org

Other Resources

Alliance for Nonprofit Management www.allianceonline.org

American Association of Grant Professionals http://go-aagp.org

Association of Fundraising Professionals www.afpnet.org

CharityChannel.com www.CharityChannel.com

Chronicle of Philanthropy www.philanthropy.com

CompassPoint www.compasspoint.org

Council on Foundations www.cof.org

Idealist www.idealist.org

Philanthropy News Network www.pnnonline.org

Women's Funding Network www.wfnet.org

Index